THE TEMPLE SCROLL AND RELATED TEXTS

Companion to the Qumran Scrolls, 2

THE TEMPLE SCROLL AND RELATED TEXTS

Sidnie White Crawford

For Dan

Copyright © 2000 Sheffield Academic Press

Published by Sheffield Academic Press Ltd
Mansion House
19 Kingfield Road
Sheffield S11 9AS
England

Printed on acid-free paper in Great Britain
by The Cromwell Press
Trowbridge, Wiltshire

British Library Cataloguing in Publication Data

A catalogue record for this book is available
from the British Library

ISBN 1-84127-056-3

Contents

Preface	7
Editions, Translations and Bibliographies	8
1. Introduction:	11
The Discovery	11
Physical Description	12
2. Genre and Date of the Temple Scroll	17
1. Genre, Method and Sources	17
2. Date, Provenance and Place in the Qumran Library	24
3. The Contents of the Scroll	29
3. The Contents of the Temple Scroll	33
1. The Temple and its Courts	33
2. The Purity Regulations	42
3. The Festival Calendar	49
4. The Deuteronomic Paraphrase and the Law of the King	57
4. The Description of the New Jerusalem	66
Editions, Translations and Bibliographies	66
1. Description of the Manuscripts	68
2. The Contents of 'The Description of the New Jerusalem'	69
3. Genre, Date and Provenance	73
5. The Temple Scroll and Other Second Temple Jewish Literature	77
1. Jubilees	77
2. *Miqsat Ma'aśē ha-Torah*	78
3. Damascus Document	80
4. The Description of the New Jerusalem	82
5. Other Compositions	82
Cumulative Bibliography	88
Index of References	98
Index of Authors	103

Preface

I would like to thank the following institutions and people for their various forms of help while I was writing this *Companion*: to the staff of the Interlibrary Loan Office at the University of Nebraska-Lincoln, who processed literally hundreds of my requests; to my research assistants, Matthew Jewell and Michelle Lueders, without whose help I could not have finished as quickly as I did; to my colleagues in the department of Classics and Religious Studies at UNL, who did not call me at home while I was working; and to my editor, Philip Davies, who first invited me to contribute to this series and then waited patiently until a manuscript arrived on his desk. This book is dedicated with love to my husband, Dan D. Crawford, with whom I live in a happy and supportive academic home. His thoughtful questions, insightful comments, and help with mathematics have been of immeasurable value in the creation of this work.

Editions, Translations and Bibliographies

Critical Editions of the Hebrew Text

11QTemple[a]

Y. Yadin, *Megillat ham-Miqdāš* (*The Temple Scroll*). I. *Introduction;* II. *Text and Commentary;* III. *Plates, Text and Supplementary Plates* (Jerusalem: Israel Exploration Society, 1977) (Hebrew). The magisterial *editio princeps* of the Temple Scroll.

—*The Temple Scroll* (3 vols. and supplement; rev. edn; Jerusalem: Israel Exploration Society, 1983). The English translation of the *editio princeps*, revised by Yadin. This is the edition to which we will refer in the *Guide*.

11QTemple[b]

F. García Martínez, E.J.C. Tigchelaar and A.S. van der Woude, '11QTemple[b]', in *idem, Qumran Cave 11, II: 11Q2-18, 11Q20-31* (DJD, 23; Oxford: Clarendon Press, 1998), pp. 357-410, pls. xli-xlvii.

11QTemple[c]?

F. García Martínez, E.J.C. Tigchelaar and A.S. van der Woude, '11QTemple[c]?', in *idem, Qumran Cave 11, II: 11Q2-18, 11Q20-31* (DJD, 23; Oxford: Clarendon Press, 1998), pp. 411-14, pl. xlviii.

4QRouleau du Temple

E. Puech, '4QRouleau du Temple', in *idem, Qumrân Grotte 4, XVIII: Textes Hébreux (4Q521-4Q528, 4Q576-4Q579)* (DJD, 25; Oxford: Clarendon Press, 1998), pp. 85-114, pls. vii-viii.

4QTemple?

S. White, '4QTemple?', in H. Attridge, T. Elgvin, *et al.* (eds.), *Qumran Cave 4, VIII: Parabiblical Texts Part 1* (DJD, 13; Oxford: Clarendon Press, 1994), pp. 319-334, pls. xxxiii-xxxiv.

Other Editions

F. García Martínez and E.J.C. Tigchelaar, '4Q365a', '4Q524', '11Q19' and '11Q20', in *idem, The Dead Sea Scrolls Study Edition* (2 vols.; Leiden: E.J. Brill, 1998), II, pp. 722-25, 1050-53, 1228-89, 1290-1305.

E. Qimron with a bibliography by F. García Martínez, *The Temple Scroll: A Critical Edition with Extensive Reconstructions* (Beer Sheva-Jerusalem: Ben-Gurion University of the Negev Press and Israel Exploration Society, 1996).

E. Tov with the collaboration of S. Pfann (eds.), *The Dead Sea Scrolls on Microfiche: A Comprehensive Facsimile Edition of the Texts from the Judean Desert* (Leiden: E.J. Brill,

1993), 71-72 (4QTemple?); 79 (4QRouleau du Temple); 112-123 (11QTemple^a); 43, 87-89 (11QTemple^b); 96 (11QTemple^c?).

B.Z. Wacholder, 'The Fragmentary Remains of 11QTorah (Temple Scroll), 11QTorah^b and 11QTorah^c plus 4QparaTorah Integrated with 11QTorah', *HUCA* 62 (1991), pp. 1-116.

M. Wise, *A Critical Study of the Temple Scroll from Qumran Cave 11* (SAOC, 49; Chicago, IL: University of Chicago Press, 1990).

Preliminary Editions, Descriptions and Textual Studies

11QTemple^a

B. Jongeling, 'A propos de la Colonne XXIII du Rouleau du Temple', *RQ* 10 (1979–81), pp. 593-95.

A. Lemaire, E.P.H.E., 'Nouveaux fragments du Rouleau du Temple de Qumrân', *RQ* 17 (1996), pp. 271-74.

H.A. Mink, 'Die Kol. III der Tempelrolle: Versuch einer Rekonstruktion', *RQ* 11 (1982–84), pp. 163-81.

E. Qimron, 'Column 14 of the Temple Scroll', *IEJ* 38 (1988), pp. 44-46.

—'Further New Readings in the Temple Scroll', *IEJ* 37 (1987), pp. 31-35.

—'New Readings in the Temple Scroll', *IEJ* 28 (1978), pp. 161-72.

—'The Text of the Temple Scroll', *Leshonenu* 42 (1978), pp. 136-45 (Hebrew).

—'Textual Notes on the Temple Scroll', *Tarbiz* 53 (1983), pp. 139-41 (Hebrew).

—'Three Notes on the Text of the Temple Scroll', *Tarbiz* 51 (1981–82), pp. 135-37 (Hebrew).

Y. Yadin, 'Un nouveau manuscrit de la Mer Morte: "Le Rouleau du Temple"', *CRAIBL* (1967), pp. 607-19.

—'The Temple Scroll', *Nouvelles Chrétiennes d'Israël* 18 (1967), pp. 41-48.

—'The Temple Scroll', *BA* 30 (1967), pp. 135-39.

—'The Temple Scroll', in J. Aviram (ed.), *Jerusalem through the Ages* (Jerusalem: Israel Exploration Society, 1968), pp. 72-82.

—'The Temple Scroll', in D.N. Freedman and J.C. Greenfield (eds.), *New Directions in Biblical Archaeology* (Garden City, NY: Doubleday, 1969), pp. 139-48.

—'De Tempelrol', *Spiegel historiae* 4 (1969), pp. 203-10.

—'Le Rouleau du Temple', in M. Delcor (ed.), *Qumrân: Sa piété, sa théologie et son milieu* (Paris: Duculot, 1978), pp. 115-19.

11QTemple^b

F. García Martínez, '11QTemple^b: A Preliminary Publication', in J. Trebolle Barrera and L. Vegas Montaner (eds.), *The Madrid Qumran Congress: Proceedings of the International Congress on the Dead Sea Scrolls, Madrid 18–21 March 1991* (2 vols.; Leiden: E.J. Brill, 1992), II, pp. 363-90.

L. van der Bogaard, 'Le Rouleau du Temple: quelques remarques concernant les "petits fragments"', in W. Delsman, J. Nelis, J. Peters, W. Römer, A.S. van der Woude (eds.), *Von Kanaan bis Kerala* (AOAT, 211; Kevelaer: Verlag Butzon & Bercker; Neukirchen–Vluyn: Neukirchener Verlag, 1982), pp. 285-94.

J. van der Ploeg, 'Une halakha inédite de Qumrân', in M. Delcor (ed.), *Qumrân: Sa piété, sa théologie et son milieu* (Paris: Duculot, 1978), pp. 107-13.

A.S. van der Woude, 'Ein bisher unveröffentlichtes Fragment der Tempelrolle', *RQ* 13 (1988), pp. 89-92.

M. Wise, 'A New Manuscript Join in the "Festival of Wood Offering" (Temple Scroll XXIII)', *JNES* 47 (1988), pp. 113-21.

11QTemple^c?

F. García Martínez, 'Texts from Cave 11', in D. Dimant and U. Rappaport (eds.), *The Dead Sea Scrolls: Forty Years of Research* (Leiden: E.J. Brill, 1992), pp. 18-26.

J.P.M. van der Ploeg, 'Les manuscrits de la Grotte XI de Qumrân', *RQ* 12 (1985-87), pp. 3-15.

4QRouleau du Temple

E. Puech, 'Fragments du plus ancien exemplaire du Rouleau du Temple (4Q524)', in M. Bernstein, F. García Martínez and J. Kampen (eds.), *Legal Texts and Legal Issues: Proceedings of the Second Meeting of the International Organization for Qumran Studies, Cambridge 1995. Published in Honour of J.M. Baumgarten* (STDJ, 23; Leiden: E.J. Brill, 1997), pp. 19-64.

4QTemple?

S.W. Crawford, 'Three Fragments from Qumran Cave 4 and their Relationship to the Temple Scroll', *JQR* 85 (1994), pp. 259-73.

Translations

F. García Martínez, 'El Rollo del Templo: 11QRollo del Templo^a' and 'El Rollo del Templo: 11QRollo del Templo^b', in *idem, Textos de Qumrán* (Madrid: Editorial Trotta, 1992), pp. 202-28, 228-33.

—'The Temple Scroll: 11QTemple Scroll^a', and 'The Temple Scroll: 11QTemple Scroll^b', in *idem, The Dead Sea Scrolls Translated: The Qumran Texts in English* (trans. W. Watson; Leiden: E.J. Brill, 1994), pp. 154-79, 179-84.

J. Maier, *Die Tempelrolle vom Toten Meer: Übersetzt und erläutert* (Munich: Reinhardt, 1978).

—*The Temple Scroll: An Introduction, Translation and Commentary* (trans. R. White; Sheffield: JSOT Press, 1985).

G. Vermes, 'The Temple Scroll (11QT)', in *idem, The Complete Dead Sea Scrolls in English* (New York: Penguin Books, 4th edn, 1997), pp. 190-219.

M. Wise, 'The Temple Scroll (11Q19-20)', in M. Wise, M. Abegg and E. Cook (eds.), *The Dead Sea Scrolls: A New Translation* (New York: HarperCollins, 1996), pp. 457-92.

Bibliographies

J.A. Fitzmyer, S.J., *The Dead Sea Scrolls: Major Publications and Tools for Study* (SBL Resources for Biblical Study, 20; rev. edn; Atlanta, GA: Scholars Press, 1990).

F. García Martínez, 'A Classified Bibliography', in E. Qimron, *The Temple Scroll: A Critical Edition with Extensive Reconstructions* (Beer Sheva-Jerusalem: Ben-Gurion University of the Negev Press and Israel Exploration Society, 1996), pp. 93-122.

—'El Rollo del Templo (11QTemple): Bibliografia sistemática', *RQ* 12 (1985-87), pp. 425-40.

F. García Martínez and D.W. Parry, *Bibliography of the Finds in the Desert of Judah 1970-1995* (STDJ, 19; Leiden: E.J. Brill, 1996).

A. Pinnick, Weekly up-dated on-line bibliography of the Dead Sea Scrolls 1995 to the present, *The Orion Center for the Study of the Dead Sea Scrolls and Associated Literature Website*: http://www.orion.mscc.huji.ac.il

1

INTRODUCTION

The Discovery

The story of the discovery and publication of the Temple Scroll is one of the most intriguing tales among the many associated with the Dead Sea Scrolls. In 1956, the Ta'amireh Bedouin, who had previously discovered both intact scrolls and the fragmentary remains of manuscripts in caves near the ruins of Qumran on the shores of the Dead Sea, discovered another cave which contained many scroll fragments as well as several almost intact scrolls. The cave was eventually numbered Cave 11, and most of the contents of the cave was purchased by the Palestine Archaeological Museum under the direction of Roland de Vaux. However Kando, the antiquities dealer who acted as a middle man for the Bedouin, withheld the largest and most intact scroll, no doubt hoping to increase its price. Rumors of the existence of the scroll circulated among the scholars responsible for publishing the Dead Sea Scrolls, but none of them was able to discover the truth of these rumors.

In 1960, Yigael Yadin, Israeli archaeologist, general and statesman, received a letter from a Virginia clergyman, claiming to have access to previously unknown Dead Sea Scroll manuscripts and offering to act as an agent between Yadin and the unnamed seller. Yadin saw photographs and an actual fragment, but after many months of negotiations he emerged $10,000 poorer and with only two manuscript fragments, one of which belonged to 11QPsalms[a] and the other to the Temple Scroll. There the matter stood until 1967.

June of 1967 found Yigael Yadin serving as general in the Israeli Defense Forces. After the capture of East Jerusalem by the Israelis from the Jordanians, Yadin dispatched an army officer to Bethlehem to detain Kando and discover the whereabouts of the mysterious scroll. The scroll and several related wads of fragments were discovered hidden in a shoe box beneath the floorboards in Kando's house. After extensive negotiations,

12   *The Temple Scroll and Related Texts*

Kando was compensated $105,000 for the purchase of the scroll by the State of Israel, and the mysterious scroll was at last in Yadin's hands. This scroll was the Temple Scroll.[1]

Physical Description

11QTemple[a] (11Q19)
11QTemple[a] is the largest intact scroll surviving from the caves of Qumran. It consists of 19 sheets of prepared animal skin; when unrolled, the scroll is 8.148 meters long. It was wrapped in a linen cloth before being placed in Cave 11. Seven of the sheets have three inscribed columns, and ten sheets have four columns. The beginning of the first sheet is missing, while the last is completely blank. The scroll is badly damaged from its years under the floorboards; the first several columns (2–13) are extant only in fragments, while the top and sides of the remaining columns (14–66) are missing or damaged. The damage made deciphering the scroll very difficult; often words were preserved only because they had rubbed off onto the back of the inner column (thus in 'mirror-image'). Therefore, there are many lacunae and conjectural readings (for a discussion of the difficulties of decipherment, see Yadin 1983: I, 5-8, and Qimron 1996: 2).

The scroll, written in unpointed Hebrew, was copied by two scribes, Scribe A copying cols. 1–5 and Scribe B the rest of the scroll. Yadin dated the script of Scribe B to 25 BCE–25 CE, that of Scribe A slightly later. Thus, it seems clear that Scribe A was copying and replacing a damaged sheet at the beginning of the scroll; this first sheet, being on the outside of the rolled-up scroll, would have received the most wear and tear. In fact, the last part of column 5 (Scribe A) overlaps with the first part of column 6 (Scribe B), indicating that Scribe A was adding his sheet to an already-existing scroll. For an extensive discussion of the orthography, language and physical layout of 11QTemple[a], see Yadin 1983: I, 9-39. For an outline of the contents of 11QTemple[a], see Chapter 2.

11QTemple[b] (11Q20)
11QTemple[b] is a second, very fragmentary manuscript of the Temple Scroll found in Cave 11. It consists of 43 fragments, which García Martínez has arranged into 15 columns. There are nine or ten columns missing before the first preserved column, and eight columns missing at the end of the manuscript. The paleographic date of the handwriting is 2–50 CE; the scroll was copied by the same scribe who copied 1QpesherHabakkuk, thus

1. For a highly readable account of the intrigue in his own words, see Yadin 1985.

1. Introduction: The Discovery

making it probable that 11QTemple[b] was copied at Qumran. There are additions and corrections made to the manuscript in different hands.

11QTemple[b] and 11QTemple[a] are essentially copies of the same work, although 11QTemple[b] contains a number of supplements to 11QTemple[a], leading García Martínez to suggest it be called another 'edition' rather than an exact copy of the same work (1992a: 390). 11QTemple[b] parallels 11QTemple[a] in the following places (some of the material is reconstructed; see García Martínez, Tigchelaar and van der Woude 1998: 363):

11QTemple[b]	*11QTemple[a]*
Col. 1 (frags. 1, 2)	15.03–16.04
Col. 2 (frags. 3 i, 4)	16.1-3, 8-11
Col. 3 (frags. 3 ii, 5, 6, 7)	17.13, 18.4-7, 19.2-9
Col. 4 (frags. 8, 9)	19.12–20.10, 13-16
Col. 5 (frags. 10 i, 11)	21.01–22.5
Col. 6 (frags. 10 ii, 12)	22.6–23.01, 05-5
Col. 8 (frag. 14)	31.11-13
Col. 9 (frags. 15, 16)	32.10-15
Col. 10 (frag. 17)	37.9–38.01
Col. 11 (frags. 18, 19, 20)	45.03-04, 1-4
Col. 12 (frags. 21 i, 22, 23, 24)	45.9–46.16
Col. 13 (frags. 21 ii, 25)	46.16–47.3
Col. 14 (frags. 26 i, 27, 28, 29)	50.02-11, 15–51.1
Col. 15 (frag. 26 ii)	51.5-17
Col. 16 (frag. 30)	54.19–55.06

Column 7, frag. 13, has no overlap with 11QTemple[a], but may correspond to missing material from the tops of cols. 24–29. There are 13 unidentified fragments in the manuscript.

11QTemple[c]? (11Q21)

11QTemple[c]? consists of three small fragments, which are dated paleographically to c. 50 CE. Its status as a third Cave 11 copy of the Temple Scroll is not certain; frag. 1 overlaps with 11QTemple[a], col. 3.14-17, but frags. 2 and 3 contain no overlaps with any other manuscript of the Temple Scroll. However, frag. 3 contains the phrases 'to come to my city' (l. 2), 'in the entire sanctuary' (l. 4), and 'sanctuary' (l. 5), pointing to at least a similar subject and phraseology as the Temple Scroll. Qimron suggests that frag. 3 should be located at the beginning of col. 48 of the Temple Scroll (1996: 69).

4QRouleau du Temple (4Q524)

4QRouleau du Temple (4QRT) is a very important manuscript of the Temple Scroll, since it is the oldest surviving copy and the only certain copy to emerge from Cave 4, the main storage place of the Qumran community. Its editor, E. Puech, puts its paleographic date at 150–25 BCE, at least one hundred years earlier than 11QTemple^a. This date will be very important when we attempt to determine the date of composition of the Temple Scroll (Chapter 2). 4QRouleau du Temple consists of 39 fragments, most of which overlap with 11QTemple^a, and one with 11QTemple^b. The parallels are as follows:

4QRouleau du Temple	11QTemple^a	11QTemple^b
Frag. 1	35.7	
Frag. 2	50.17-21	17.2-4
Frag. 3	54.5	
Frag. 4	55.11-13	
Frag. 5	58.10-13	
Frags. 6-13	59.17–60.6	
Frag. 14	64.6-11	
Frags. 15-22	66.8-17	
Frag. 23	49.06-07?	

The manuscript also contains 16 unidentified fragments.

4QRouleau du Temple does not have an identical text to 11QTemple^a. Fragment 14 has a different text than 11QTemple^a; in line 5 4QRT ends with 'for you shall indeed bury them on that day' (Deut. 21.23a) and does not contain the text found in 11QTemple^a, cols. 64.11b–65.07, but instead skips to Deut. 22.11 and continues from there (col. 65.07, according to Yadin's reconstruction). Further, frags. 15-22, which begin by corresponding to the end of 11QTemple^a (col. 66.8-17), continue on with more regulations for interdicted and permitted marriages, ending with the rule for levirate marriage (Deut. 25.5-9). According to the editor, the text of 4QRT would not fit into the space available at the top of 11QTemple^a's col. 67, before the uninscribed leather. Therefore, it is clear that 4QRT and 11QTemple^a contained different texts. What is more, the fact that 4QRT contains no overlaps with cols. 2–34 and 36–48, and only a very small overlap with col. 35, makes it difficult to be certain that all of those columns appeared in 4QRT (most of the preserved fragments of 4QRT parallel the Deuteronomic Paraphrase; notice especially that none of the Festival Calendar source, cols. 13–29 [see Chapter 2], survives). Thus, it is very likely that 4QRT represents an earlier edition of the Temple Scroll, perhaps in part substantially different (if in fact the Festival Calendar was missing). This original version of the Temple Scroll then underwent further editing (at Qumran?) to produce what we now know as the Temple Scroll preserved in 11QTemple^a.

4QTemple? (4Q365a)
The five fragments of 4QTemple? have long been a puzzle. When the first sorting of the Cave 4 fragments was done, they were tentatively identified

as a Hebrew manuscript of the New Jerusalem text. They were later reidentified by their original editor, J. Strugnell, as part of 4QReworked Pentateuch^c (4Q365). They were, in fact, copied by the same scribe as 4QReworked Pentateuch^c (4QRP^c), and therefore are dated by paleography to c. 125–75 BCE. The fragments were then removed from 4QRP^c by their final editors, E. Tov and this author, and tentatively identified as a copy of the Temple Scroll or a source(s) of the Temple Scroll (White 1994: 319-20). Yadin, Wacholder and Qimron used some of the fragments in their reconstructions of the Temple Scroll (Yadin 1983: III, supplementary plates 38*, #5, 40*, #2; Wacholder 1991: 111; Qimron 1996: 4-5).

The five fragments contain material related to the subject matter of the Temple Scroll, and in one case parallel text to 11QTemple^a. Fragment 1 contains regulations for the Feast of Unleavened Bread. Fragment 2, cols. i and ii has a text that is parallel to 11QTemple^a, cols. 38 and 41, containing commands concerning the courts of the Temple. Close examination proves, however, that the text of 4QTemple? is not identical to 11QTemple^a, but reflects a shorter recension. Fragments 3 and 4 contain architectural specifications for some of the structures of the courtyards. The content of frag. 5, cols. i and ii is not easy to ascertain, but involves a structure with wheels (cf. 1 Kgs 7.30-33; Ezek. 1.15-21). Fragments 1, 3-5 of 4QTemple? cannot be satisfactorily located in any part of 11QTemple^a, and the one fragment (frag. 2) which can be fit into the content of 11QTemple^a is only a partial parallel. Therefore it is unlikely that this fragmentary material represents another copy of the Temple Scroll; it is more likely to be part of the source material that was used in the redaction of the Temple Scroll.[2]

In sum, the three certain copies of the Temple Scroll show that the oldest, 4QRT, was copied before the foundation of the Qumran community (c. 135–100 BCE); the Cave 11 copies were made over a century later, during Period II of the settlement (de Vaux 1973). The three manuscripts, at least in their extant material, are essentially copies of the same work, although both 4QRT and 11QTemple^b show evidence of being different editions. Further, because 4QRT is so fragmentary, it is impossible to know whether or not it contained all of the sections found in 11QTemple^a.

For the purposes of this Guide, I will choose 11QTemple^a as the most complete edition of the Temple Scroll, and base my remarks upon it, referring to the other manuscripts only where appropriate. The reader should therefore understand that when the Temple Scroll is referred to in

---

2. This is a stronger position than I have taken in previous publications; see the pertinent remarks of Puech 1997: 50, 55-56.

the remaining chapters, 11QTemple^a is meant. Yadin's English translation has been used throughout the Guide, with any modifications noted. All biblical translations have followed the New Revised Standard Version (NRSV).

2
GENRE AND DATE OF THE TEMPLE SCROLL

1. Genre, Method and Sources

a. Genre

The genre of the Temple Scroll defies neat categorization. It has been called a pseudepigraph, a *sēper tôrāh* (Book of the Law) and a 'Rewritten Bible'. All of these categories are, in one sense or another, correct, but all of them are necessary to capture the full flavor of the Scroll.

One of the most striking features of the Temple Scroll is its pseudepigraphical character. The practice of pseudepigraphy (the attribution of a contemporary composition to an ancient sage such as Enoch, Daniel or Moses, usually achieved by setting the work in the hoary past) was well-established in the Second Temple period. However, the Temple Scroll is perhaps the most audacious pseudepigraph of all; the speaker is God himself! The narrative of the Scroll is couched in the first person singular throughout (with minor lapses); the author/redactor achieves this by substituting אני (*ʾănî*) and אנוכי (*ʾănôkî*) for third person references to God, and by changing the verb forms. For example, in col. 55.11-14 we find:

11. למען אשוב מחרון אפי ונתתי לכה
12. רחמים ורחמתיכה והרביתיכה כאשר דברתי לאבותיכה
13. אם תשמע בקולי לשמור כול מצוותי אשר אנוכי מצוכה
14. היום לעשות הישר והטוב לפני יהוה אלוהיכה

11. ... that I may turn from the fierceness of my anger, and show you
12. mercy, and have compassion on you, and multiply you, as I swore to your fathers,
13. if you obey my voice, keeping all my commandments which I command you
14. this day, and doing what is right and good in the sight of the Lord your God.

This is a paraphrase of Deut. 13.18b-19 (with minor variations):

לעמן ישוב יהוה מחרון אפו ונתן לך רחמים ורחמך והרבך כאשר נשבע לאבתיך
כי תשמע בקול יהוה אלהיך לשמר את כל מצותיו אשר אנכי מצוך היום לעשות
הישר בעיני יהוה אלהיך

> ...in order that the LORD your God may turn from his anger and show you mercy and have compassion on you and multiply you, as he swore to your fathers: if you obey the voice of the LORD your God, obeying all his commandments which I [Moses] am commanding today, doing what is right in the sight of the LORD your God.

The addressee of God's discourse is Moses on Mt Sinai. This is made plain by two passages; col. 44.5 reads 'you shall all[ot] to the sons of Aaron, *your brother*' (emphasis mine), while col. 51.6-7 reads 'which I tell you on this mountain'. Aaron is, of course, the brother of Moses, and the mountain where God speaks to Moses is Mt Sinai.

The purpose of this 'divine fiction' becomes clear when we consider the Temple Scroll as a *sēper tôrāh*. That the Scroll is a law book is transparent from its content and its setting. Column 2, the end of the introduction to the Scroll, is using Exodus 34 as its biblical base. Exodus 34.1-2 depicts God commanding Moses to ascend Mt Sinai a second time, to receive again the covenantal law which was broken during the golden calf incident (Exod. 32.1-20). Thus the setting of the Scroll is covenantal; the reader is meant to understand its laws as those given to Moses during his second sojourn on the mountain. The fact that the Temple Scroll contains legal material not found in the canonical Torah would seem to call into question this setting. But the status of the extra-biblical legislation in the Scroll is precisely the concern of the author/redactor. As Schiffman puts it, 'one of the fundamental issues in Second Temple Judaism was that of how to incorporate extra-biblical traditions and teachings into the legal system, and how to justify them theologically' (Schiffman 1989b: 240-41). The Pharisees (and the later rabbis) solved the problem by claiming the existence of an oral Torah, given by God to Moses on Mt Sinai alongside the written one, which had been passed down through the generations of sages. The author/redactor of the Temple Scroll, on the other hand, solves the problem by assimilating the extra-biblical traditions into his new Book of the Law and claiming it to be part of the Sinai revelation. How he accomplishes this assimilation brings us to the category of Rewritten Bible.

The term 'Rewritten Bible' refers to a text that has a close narrative attachment to some book contained in the present Jewish canon of Scripture, and some type of reworking, through rearrangement, conflation, omission or supplementation of the present canonical biblical text (Vermes 1989: 185-88). This rewriting usually had an exegetical purpose; the pro-

2. Genre and Date of the Temple Scroll

cess begins in the period of the First Temple, when Deuteronomy reuses the old legal materials now embedded in Exodus, Leviticus and Numbers to create a new work with a distinctive theological perspective.[1] The definition of Rewritten Bible assumes that the author/composer/redactor had before him a biblical text which would have been recognizable to us and to his audience. However, it should be remembered that the text of the books of the Hebrew Bible in the Second Temple period was not fixed, but fluid. That is, a certain amount of variation in the manuscripts of a particular biblical book was both expected and accepted. Variations could be quite small, as is illustrated by the manuscripts of Deuteronomy, or large enough to cause the creation of two or more separate editions, as in the book of Jeremiah. These variants among the ancient manuscripts did not affect the authority of the particular text. So it should be understood that, even before any deliberate rewriting took place, scribal interventions and errors had given rise to a variety of biblical texts which fell along a spectrum of 'short' to 'expanded' texts. (In the Pentateuch, the Masoretic Text would be an example of a shorter text, while the Samaritan Pentateuch is an example of an expanded one.) It is this very fluidity which lends itself to exegesis through rewriting; this process is distinct from the biblical commentary form, in which a clear distinction is made between the biblical passage and the remarks of the commentator (at Qumran, the commentary is represented by such compositions as Pesher Habakkuk and Pesher Nahum). The type of inner-biblical exegesis found in the Rewritten Bible texts is not a case of 'pious fraud'; it is probable that the individual interpreter was simply attempting to give written form to what he perceived as divinely inspired revelation achieved through exegesis (Fishbane 1986: 20, 35). The Temple Scroll fits well into the category of Rewritten Bible; it is closely related to the text of the now-canonical Pentateuch, beginning with the command to build a sanctuary in Exodus 34 and proceeding in the basic order of the Torah, ending with Deuteronomy. The Temple Scroll, however, extensively reworks its base text, producing what is in effect a new book of the Law. The method of reworking used by the author/redactor is our next topic.

b. Method and Sources

It is immediately evident upon even a cursory perusal of the Temple Scroll that its author/redactor had an expert knowledge of the Pentateuch and other biblical texts, which he uses to create his new *sēper tôrāh*. Yadin categorized five ways in which the author/redactor reworked the biblical text (Yadin 1983: I, 71-88).

---

1. For a thorough discussion of this phenomenon, see Fishbane 1985.

1. The formulation of the text in the first person (discussed above).

2. Merging commands on the same subject. The general structure of the Temple Scroll is arrangement by principal themes; the author/redactor took the occasion of the first occurrence of a topic to group together all the laws concerning that topic scattered throughout the Pentateuch. An obvious example of this is the laws of incest found in col. 66 (see below, Chapter 3).

3. Unifying duplicate commands (harmonization). If laws appearing in different parts of the Pentateuch but concerning a single topic appear to differ or even contradict each other (a phenomenon the modern critic would explain through source or redaction criticism), the Temple Scroll harmonizes them or brings them into accord with one another. Two examples will make this process clear:

a. Cols. 52.10-12 and 53.4-6 present laws concerning non-sacral slaughter.

> Within your towns you shall eat it; the unclean and the clean among you alike may eat it, as though it were a gazelle or a hart. Only you shall not eat its blood; you shall pour it upon the earth like water, and cover it with dust (52.10-12).

> And you shall eat in your towns, the clean and the unclean among you alike, as though it were a gazelle or a hart. Only be sure that you do not eat the blood; you shall pour it out upon the earth like water, and cover it with dust (53.4-6).

The biblical base texts for these commands are Deut. 12.22-24 and Lev. 17.13:

> Indeed, just as gazelle or deer is eaten, so you may eat it; the unclean and the clean alike may eat it. Only be sure that you do not eat the blood; for the blood is the life, and you shall not eat the life with the meat. Do not eat it; you shall pour it out on the ground like water (Deut. 12.22-24).

> And anyone of the people of Israel, or of the aliens who reside among them, who hunts down an animal or bird that may be eaten shall pour out its blood and cover it with earth (Lev. 17.13).

Deuteronomy is discussing the slaughter and eating of domestic animals, which it likens to hunted animals; the blood must be poured out on the ground 'like water'. Leviticus is discussing hunted animals, for whom the blood must be poured out *and* covered with earth. The commands in the Temple Scroll brings those two requirements together for any non-sacral slaughter.

b. The 'law of booty' is found in col. 58.11-15:

> And if they are victorious over their enemies, and break them, and smite them with the sword, and carry away their booty, they shall give from it to

the king his tenth, and to the priests one of a thousand, and to the Levites one of the hundred of the total, and they shall halve the remaining between the warriors who went out to battle and their brothers whom they stationed in their cities.

How were the percentages for the king, the priests, the Levites and the rest arrived at? The Temple Scroll is working from two biblical texts concerning booty which differ from one another, Num. 31.27-30 and 1 Sam. 30.24-25.

> Divide the booty into two parts, between the warriors who went out to battle and all the congregation. From the share of the warriors who went out to battle, set aside as tribute for the LORD, one item out of every five hundred, whether persons, oxen, donkeys, sheep or goats. Take it from their half and give it to Eleazar the priest as an offering to the LORD. But from the Israelites' half you shall take one out of every fifty, whether persons, oxen, donkeys, sheep, or goats—all the animals—and give them to the Levites who have charge of the tabernacle of the LORD (Num. 31.27-30).

> 'For the share of the one who goes down into the battle shall be the same as the share of the one who stays by the baggage; they shall share alike'. From that day forward he [David] made it a statute and an ordinance for Israel; it continues to the present day (1 Sam. 30.24-25).

David's rule does not provide for the priest and the Levite. So, according to Yadin, the author/redactor synthesizes the two passages:

> 'first, the tenth for the king is to be set aside, and then the priests are to be given 'one of a thousand ... /*of the total*' (that is five hundredths of the half), and the Levites are to be given 'one of the hundred/ *of the total*' (that is, one fiftieth of the half). Only *thereafter* is the portion that is left to be divided equally between those 'who went out to battle' and those 'whom they stationed in their cities'. In this way, the author fulfills the command 'they shall share alike' (Yadin 1983: I, 361).

4. *Modifications and additions for clarification.* This is a dominant feature of the Scroll. Some of these changes are quite small, but revealing of the ideology of the Scroll. For example, in the law concerning the Beautiful Captive Woman, the phrase 'but she shall not touch your pure stuff for seven years, and she shall not eat a sacrifice of peace offering until seven years shall pass; only then may she eat', is added to the Pentateuchal base text. It betrays the author/redactor's concern for purity requirements. It is important to determine, when studying these additions or modifications, whether or not the variant was already present in the author/redactor's base text. If the variant was already in the base text, it cannot be used as an example of the Temple Scroll's exegesis.[2]

2. Although a complete study of the textual criticism of the Temple Scroll has not

5. Appending whole new sections. Large blocks and small pieces of new material appear in the Temple Scroll, for example the Law of the King in cols. 57–59. Some of them may have been composed by the author/redactor of the Temple Scroll, while some may have come from his sources. On the use of sources, see below.

Other scholars would label the various methods of reworking the biblical text slightly differently. Milgrom discusses four types of 'Qumranic exegesis' found in the Temple Scroll: (1) conflation or unification, the fusion of the various laws on a single subject into one law; (2) harmonization; (3) homogenization or equalization, in which a law which applies to specific objects, animals or persons is extended to other members of the same species; and (4) application, where, when a law is no longer applicable as written it is applied to a successor set of circumstances (Milgrom 1993-94: 449-50; 1989: 171). Swanson, approaching the problem differently, does not distinguish between various types of exegesis, but discusses the use of the biblical text in developing the laws of the Temple Scroll. According to Swanson, the Scroll 'combines biblical texts by establishing a primary text... and supplementing this with texts which change the base texts in some way' (Swanson 1995: 14, 215). However the Scroll's methods are categorized, what emerges are new regulations out of the old, placed in God's mouth, given to Moses on Mt Sinai and therefore to be considered divinely inspired. Callaway has aptly named this process 'extending divine revelation' (Callaway 1988: 249).

Although Yadin in the *editio princeps* treated the Temple Scroll as a unified composition, he hinted at the possibility that there were sources behind the final form of the Temple Scroll (Yadin 1983: I, 386, 390). The first full-scale study which discerned sources in the Temple Scroll was that of Andrew Wilson and Lawrence Wills (1982: 275-88). Wilson and Wills posited five separate sources in the Temple Scroll, stitched together by an author/redactor:

1. Temple and Courts (cols. 2.1–13.8; 30.3–47.18).
2. Calendar (cols. 13.9–30.2).
3. Purity Laws (col. 48.1–51.10).
4. Laws of Polity (cols. 51.11–56.21; 60.1–66.17).
5. Torah of the King (cols. 57–59).

yet been completed, it is clear that the author/redactor of the Temple Scroll had before him a text (or texts) of the Pentateuch which demonstrated textual variation from the Masoretic Text. The most complete study up til now is that of Tov, who says, 'the scroll contains a textual tradition which agrees now and then with one or another of these early [biblical] texts' (Tov 1982: 100-111).

They determined these sources by observing the person of God (first or third person) and the person of the addressee (second masculine singular or second masculine plural); the grammatical forms, distinguishing between those sections which used an unconverted imperfect and those which used an imperfect plus a participle; vocabulary; and form-critical features. They proposed that the Temple Scroll was composed in two stages: the proto-Temple Scroll, which consisted of the Temple and Courts source followed by legal material from Deuteronomy, all composed in the first person divine fiction, followed by a second stage in which a redactor added the festival calendar and the purity laws.

Their basic source division (although not their stages of composition) have been accepted with refinements by most scholars, a notable exception being Wacholder, who argues for unity of composition (1983: 16-17). The most extensive critique of Wilson and Wills has been done by Michael Wise (1990a). Wise finds four major sources in the Temple Scroll:

1. The Temple Source (cols. 3.1–13.8; 30.3–31.9a; 31.10–34.12a; 34.15–35.9a; 35.10–39.5a; 39.11b–40.5; 40.7–43.12a; 44.1–45.7a; 46.1-11a; 46.13–47.2)
2. Festival Calendar and the Laws (cols. 13.8–30.2, in which 29.2–30.2 is a redactional conclusion). Wise proposes that the Festival Calendar once circulated separately.
3. Deuteronomy Source (cols. 2.1-15; 48.1-10a; 51.11-18; 52.1-12; 53.1–56.21; 60.12–63.14a; 64.1-6a; 64.13b–66.9b; 66.10-12a). This is not the book of Deuteronomy, but a collection of laws drawn from Deuteronomy.
4. Midrash to Deuteronomy (cols. 57.1–59.21; 60.2-11; 64.6b-13a)

Wise's conclusions have not found widespread acceptance, most scholars preferring instead a more subtle refinement of Wilson and Wills' theory. Thus, column 2 should be removed from the Temple and Courts source, since it serves as an introduction to the Scroll as a whole. The Temple and Courts source and the Festival Calendar source are otherwise left intact, although the hand of the redactor is recognized within them. The Laws of Polity remains as well, although it should be renamed the Deuteronomic Paraphrase. The Torah or Law of the King remains as a separate source within the Deuteronomic Paraphrase; it is probable that it circulated on its own before being inserted into the Paraphrase. Finally, the existence of a separate 'Purity Source' has been called into the greatest question (see Callaway 1985–87: 213-22). It seems likely that a Purity Source as such never existed independently; rather, the author/redactor of the Temple Scroll had before him a series of collections of purity laws, which he used freely when redacting together his sources; the greatest concentration of these purity laws is found in cols. 48–51.

2. Date, Provenance and Place in the Qumran Library

a. Date and Provenance

The question of the date of composition and provenance (place of composition) of the Temple Scroll has been a difficult one since its publication by Yadin. There have been essentially two schools of thought concerning date of composition: the first claimed that the Scroll was composed in the late second–early first century BCE. This dating was primarily based on the regulations concerning kingship in the Deuteronomic Paraphrase, which, it was argued, were a polemic against the Hasmonaean rulers, particularly John Hyrcanus I (135–104 BCE) and Alexander Jannaeus (103–76 BCE). This view was first proposed by Yadin and championed by Hengel, Charlesworth and Mendels (Yadin 1983: I, 388-90; Hengel, Charlesworth and Mendels 1986: 28-38; see also Schiffman 1987: 237-59).The second school of thought dated the composition of the Temple Scroll before the founding of the Qumran community (c. 135 BCE). A wide range of dates was proposed, ranging from the late fifth century BCE (Stegemann) to no later than 125 BCE (Maier) (Stegemann 1989: 123-48; Wacholder 1983: 204; Maier 1985: 2).

The question of provenance has yielded more unanimity. Yadin argued that not only was the Scroll copied and preserved at Qumran, but it was composed there and reflected the ideology of the sect at Qumran, identified by Yadin with the Essenes (1983: I, 388-90). Levine was the first to challenge that identification, arguing that the Temple Scroll did not have the specific characteristics of a Qumran sectarian document, such as the special language of predestination, dualism or eschatology, but rather fell into the category of 'writings preserved by a sect and considered important by it' (Levine 1978: 7). Since then, a majority of scholars have followed Levine, either considering the Temple Scroll pre-Qumranic and thus not a product of the sect (Stegemann 1989: 128; Callaway 1988: 245-50) or non-Qumranic and brought to Qumran from the outside (Schiffman 1994a: 258).

The publication of 4QRouleau du Temple by E. Puech in 1998 sheds new light on these questions. Puech dates the copying of these fragments to c. 150 BCE, thus before the founding of the Qumran community. The fragments preserved come from a manuscript which Puech argues was not a source for the Temple Scroll, but an actual copy of it (Puech 1998: 86). The remains of 4QRT parallel cols. 35 and 50–66 of 11QTemple[a], which

2. Genre and Date of the Temple Scroll

have been identified with two different sources, plus the work of the author/redactor (the Temple Source and the Deuteronomic Paraphrase, including the Law of the King; the Purity collection). Although there are differences between 4QRT and 11QTemple[a], these should be attributed to different editions of the same composition, rather than different compositions. Therefore, the *terminus ante quem* for the composition of the earlier edition of the Temple Scroll must be c. 150 BCE. The question of provenance is thus resolved; the earlier edition of the Temple Scroll must be a pre-Qumranic document, preserved at Qumran because of its affinities to the ideology of the sect. Some of these affinities, including parallels with Qumran sectarian writings, will be noted in Chapter 3 and extensively discussed in Chapter 5. The fact that the Temple Scroll was copied at Qumran nearly a century after 4QRT was copied (11QTemple[a], 25 BCE–25 CE; 11QTemple[b], 20–50 CE) may indicate that its subject matter was interpreted as pertaining to contemporary events: the excesses of the Hasmonaean and Herodian kings, the rebuilding of the Temple by Herod, the ascendancy of the Pharisees in matters of cult and purity regulations.

The absolute dating of the composition of the Temple Scroll is still unresolved. There are at least two issues which must be taken into account: the Scroll's relationship to 1 and 2 Chronicles and its relation to *Jubilees*. D. Swanson has argued extensively for the Temple Scroll's use of 1 and 2 Chronicles (1995: esp. 237-39). Stegemann has attempted to argue instead that the Temple Scroll only knew traditions that lie behind 1 and 2 Chronicles (Stegemann 1989: 146 n. 24). Swanson's case, however, for the Temple Scroll's use of the written form of 1 and 2 Chronicles seems good, so if the Chronicler was writing in the later Persian period (late fifth–fourth centuries BCE), this is the *terminus post quem* for the sources of the Temple Scroll.

Likewise, if the Temple Scroll is dependent on the book of *Jubilees*, the composition of the Temple Scroll must be later than that of *Jubilees* (mid-second century BCE). The Temple Scroll and the book of *Jubilees* share a remarkable set of affinities (see below, Chapters 3 and 5), but also several points of disagreement. Therefore, it is difficult to argue that one is dependent upon the other; it is more prudent to observe that the two authors are drawing upon the same cultic, exegetical tradition (VanderKam 1989: 232). The date of the book of *Jubilees*, then, cannot help to fix the date of composition for the Temple Scroll, except to suggest that the two works may be close contemporaries.

A third consideration may be the language of the Scroll. Although it is composed in a 'biblicizing' style, a major feature of the Scroll is the use of compound verbs, a feature of late biblical and Mishnaic Hebrew (Yadin 1983: I, 34). Yadin also notes other linguistic features of the Scroll which point to later composition: the use of late biblical Hebrew grammar and vocabulary, technical vocabulary common to the Mishnah, and words borrowed from Persian (Yadin 1983: I, 35-38). All of these features would tend to place the Scroll in the second half of the Second Temple period. On the other hand, a lack of Greek vocabulary would argue against a date much later than 175 BCE (Maier 1985: 2).

All of these factors unfortunately do not add up to much. If the Temple Scroll (or its sources) relied upon the Chronicler, it must have been composed after 350 BCE. Its earliest copy dates to 150 BCE; therefore the date of composition must fall between 350–175 BCE. The sources would have been composed earlier in that time frame, with the final redaction of the Temple Scroll occurring around 200–175 BCE (see Puech 1997: 63, and García Martínez 1999: 444, for a similar dating).

The search for the identification of the author/redactor of the Temple Scroll has met with even less success than the search for a date. Yadin, Wacholder and Wise have all proposed the Teacher of Righteousness as the author (Yadin 1985: 288; Wacholder 1983: 204; Wise 1990a: 184); however, we know so little about this shadowy figure that it is difficult to marshall a convincing case for his authorship of anything (cf., e.g., Murphy-O'Connor 1992: 340-41)! More modest suggestions that the Temple Scroll is a product of scribal activity within priestly circles (Brooke 1992b: 282), or even more specifically from disaffected levitical priestly circles (Mink 1987: 28) carry more merit, since the author/redactor of the Scroll and the compilers of its sources had to possess vast knowledge of the Torah, the Temple and its cult. A priestly milieu would seem the most reasonable location for such knowledge.

b. Place in the Qumran Library

If the Temple Scroll is a pre-Qumranic document, its place in the Qumran library must be explained. First, the author/redactor's purpose in compiling the Temple Scroll should be ascertained. That the author considered the now-canonical Torah to be divinely inspired is beyond doubt, since it serves as the basis for his own divinely inspired text.[3] That the Temple

---

3. It should be emphasized that during the period under discussion, 'the canon' of the Jews did not exist. The acceptance of a canon or list of authoritative books by a religious community implies that those books outside the canon were not divinely inspired or authoritative; no such hard and fast distinction existed in Second Temple Judaism. Thus, while all Jews accepted the Torah or Five Books of Moses as authoritative, and most accepted the Prophets, the category now known as the Writings was still fluid and open to question. Further, books which are now non-canonical, such as *1 Enoch* and *Jubilees*, were probably considered authoritative by at least some groups of Jews in the Second Temple period.

2. Genre and Date of the Temple Scroll

Scroll was meant to be a *sēper tôrāh*, a Book of the Law, is also beyond doubt. But was it meant to be *a* Book of the Law, or *the* Book of the Law? In other words, was it meant to add to or supplement the Pentateuch, or supercede it? Yadin argued that the author/redactor meant his Scroll to be understood as a 'veritable Torah of the Lord' (Yadin 1983: I, 392), but not necessarily as a replacement for the already existing Torah. Wacholder, on the other hand, argued that the author's purpose was to present the reader with another Torah delivered by God himself, and thus more authoritative than its Mosaic archetype (Wacholder 1983: 4). It seems unlikely, however, that the author/redactor considered the Temple Scroll to abrogate the Torah, since the Torah contains both narrative and legal material not covered in his text. A good example of this is the Decalogue (Exod. 20; Deut. 5), which does not appear in the Temple Scroll but certainly continued to be considered part of the Law of God! Thus, it seems that the author/redactor wished his text to be viewed as an expression of the will of God (Torah) as revealed in the Pentateuch on particular aspects of Israel's cult and daily life; he achieved this through his particular brand of exegesis (Schiffman 1989b: 88; García Martínez 1999: 439). The Temple Scroll is thus not meant to supercede the Five Books of Moses, but to explain and supplement certain parts of it.

The particular aspects of Israel's cult and daily life which the Temple Scroll addressed are the physical Temple, its furnishings and courts; the festivals and sacrificial cult, with special attention given to the role of the Levites; issues of purity and impurity; the rights and duties of kingship; and regulations concerning daily life in the land. All of these issues are discussed in detail in Chapter 3. The overall tone of the document is irenic, not polemical. Yadin noted that many of the issues addressed in the Temple Scroll surfaced in later rabbinic discussions, and that the rabbis often attributed to the Pharisees, and took themselves, positions which disagreed with the Scroll. Yadin therefore concluded that the Scroll was written as a polemic against already existing positions and practices (see, e.g., his discussion in Yadin 1983: I, 96-99, concerning the Passover regulations). However, it is more likely that the Scroll is purposeful rather than polemical; when it gives extensive and precise legislation for a particular issue, the author/redactor is laying out his own position concerning a question of law (Mink 1987: 50). That he considered his position the correct one goes without saying; that these positions were not generally accepted and in fact became areas of sharp controversy later is likewise beyond question. Contrast, for example, the tone of the Temple Scroll and that of the Damascus Document on the question of uncle–niece marriage:

> A man shall not take his brother's daughter or his sister's daughter, for it is an abomination (col. 66.16-17).

> And each man takes as a wife the daughter of his brother and the daughter of his sister. But Moses said: 'Do not approach your mother's sister, she is a blood relation of your mother'. The law of incest, written for males, applies equally to females, and therefore to the daughter of a brother who uncovers the nakedness of the brother of her father, for he is a blood relation (CD 5.7-11).

Both texts present a position completely at variance with what we know was the practice of the Pharisees, who encouraged uncle–niece marriage (Yadin 1983: I, 372). The tone of the Damascus Document is sharper, however, and indicates a more intense controversy.

Some of the Temple Scroll's positions were obviously different from the historical practices of the first half of the second century BCE. To take only the most obvious example, the plan of the Temple and its courts called for by the Temple Scroll bears little resemblance to the actual Second Temple. However, it is probable that the author/redactor hoped that once the will of God was revealed in his text, steps would be taken to correct the errors evident in the Second Temple and its cult. The Temple Scroll presents an ideal plan, but one meant to be undertaken by humans in historical time; it is not eschatological (contra Wacholder 1983: 21-30, and Wise 1990b: 155-72, who argue that the Temple plan is eschatological). Instead, positions hardened, controversies erupted and identifiable sects emerged in the late Second Temple period, the period in which the Temple Scroll was deposited in the caves at Qumran.

If the Temple Scroll is not sectarian, it must still have been congenial to the Qumran community, who preserved and most probably copied it. As I have argued above, since the Scroll and its sources emerged out of levitical priestly circles, it is not surprising to find in it halakhic positions later identified with the Sadducees (also a priestly group; see Baumgarten 1994: 27-36, and Schiffman 1989d: 239-55). Although the history of different groups and their halakhic positions in second century BCE Palestine is still murky, it seems likely that a group was emerging whose legal exegesis was distinct from another group later identified with the Pharisees. Schiffman has identified the first group as proto-Sadducees, since some of their legal rulings are identical to those of the Sadducees (Schiffman 1990b: 64-73). This group may be identified with other literature of the period which is not all halakhic, but which was all rejected by the heirs of the Pharisees, the rabbis: *Jubilees*, *1 Enoch*, and possibly parts of the Damascus Document. The Temple Scroll is most likely a product of this group (Boccaccini 1998: 101, who calls this movement 'Enochic Judaism'). Later in the second century BCE, a schism occurred in this group (reflected in CD 19.34-35; 20.13-15); those who retreated to Qumran took their literature with them, and produced other, sectarian literature. This Qumran group is usually identified with the Essenes (for a defense of the Essene hypothesis, see VanderKam 1994: 71-91; for a critique, see Schiffman 1994c: 83-95). If this scenario is valid, then the Temple Scroll is part of the Qumran library because it is part of the inherited literature of the sect. As such, it would have carried a certain amount of authority, but perhaps not on a par with a biblical book such as Deuteronomy (which was found at Qumran in 25 copies, as opposed to three or four of the Temple Scroll). It is significant that no unquestionable quotation of or reference to the Temple Scroll has so far appeared in the Qumran literature; this would testify to its less-than-central status at Qumran. Its importance for us lies in its ability to shed light on the interpretation of the Bible in the Second Temple period, as well as its testimony to the areas of halakhic concern and controversy in the second century BCE, which led to the formation of sectarian Judaism later in the period.

3. The Contents of the Scroll

Here follows an outline of the contents of the Temple Scroll:

Col. 2	The Covenant relationship
Cols. 3–12	The Temple building and related structures
Cols. 13–29	The Festival Calendar and regulations for the sacrificial cult
Cols. 30–44	The Temple courts and related structures
Cols. 45–47	The Sanctity of the Holy City
Cols. 48–51.10	Purity regulations
Cols. 51.11–56.11	Various laws on legal procedure, sacrifices, vows and oaths, idolatry
Cols. 56.12–59	The Law of the King
Cols. 60–67	Various laws concerning life in the land

These topics will be treated in the next chapter.

Further Reading

General Studies

F. García Martínez, 'The Temple Scroll and the New Jerusalem', in P. Flint and J. VanderKam (eds.), *The Dead Sea Scrolls after Fifty Years* (2 vols.; Leiden: E.J. Brill, 1999), II, pp. 431-60.

J. Maier, *The Temple Scroll: An Introduction, Translation, and Commentary* (trans. R.T. White; Sheffield: JSOT Press, 1985).

D. Swanson, *The Temple Scroll and the Bible: The Methodology of 11QT* (Leiden: E.J. Brill, 1995).

B.Z. Wacholder, *The Dawn of Qumran: The Sectarian Torah and the Teacher of Righteousness* (Cincinnati, OH: Hebrew Union College Press, 1983).
M. Wise, *A Critical Study of the Temple Scroll from Qumran Cave 11* (SAOC, 49; Chicago: Oriental Institute of the University of Chicago, 1990).
Y. Yadin, *The Temple Scroll* (3 vols.; Jerusalem: Israel Exploration Society, 1983).

Genre, Method and Sources
M. Bernstein, 'Midrash Halakhah at Qumran? 11QTemple 64:6-13 and Deuteronomy 21:22-23', *Gesher* 7 (1979), pp. 145-66.
G. Brooke, 'The Temple Scroll and LXX Exodus 35-40', in G. Brooke and B. Lindars (eds.), *Septuagint, Scrolls and Cognate Writings: Papers Presented to the International Symposium on the Septuagint and its Relations to the Dead Sea Scrolls and Other Writings* (Atlanta, GA: Scholars Press, 1992), pp. 81-106.
—'The Textual Tradition of the Temple Scroll and Recently Published Manuscripts of the Pentateuch', in D. Dimant and U. Rappaport (eds.), *The Dead Sea Scrolls: Forty Years of Research* (Leiden: E.J. Brill, 1992), pp. 261-82.
P. Callaway, 'Extending Divine Revelation: Micro-Compositional Strategies in the Temple Scroll', in G. Brooke (ed.), *Temple Scroll Studies: Papers Presented at the International Symposium on the Temple Scroll, Manchester, December, 1987* (Sheffield: JSOT Press, 1989), pp. 149-62.
S.W. Crawford, 'The "Rewritten Bible" at Qumran: A Look at Three Texts', *Eretz Israel* 26 (1999), pp. 1-8.
M. Fishbane, 'Inner Biblical Exegesis: Types and Strategies of Interpretation in Ancient Israel', in G. Hartman and S. Budick (eds.), *Midrash and Literature* (New Haven, CT: Yale University Press, 1986), pp. 19-40.
S. Kaufman, 'The Temple Scroll and Higher Criticism', *HUCA* 53 (1982), pp. 29-43.
J. Milgrom, 'The Qumran Cult: Its Exegetical Principles', in G. Brooke (ed.), *Temple Scroll Studies: Papers Presented at the International Symposium on the Temple Scroll, Manchester, December, 1987* (Sheffield: JSOT Press, 1989), pp. 165-80.
—'Qumran's Biblical Hermeneutics: The Case of the Wood Offering', *RQ* 16 (1993–94), pp. 449-56.
—'Studies in the Temple Scroll', *JBL* 97 (1978), pp. 501-23.
—'The Temple Scroll', *BA* 41 (1978), pp. 105-20.
H.-A. Mink, 'The Use of Scripture in the Temple Scroll and the Status of the Scroll as Law', *Scandinavian Journal of the Old Testament* 1 (1987), pp. 20-50.
L. Schiffman, 'The Deuteronomic Paraphrase of the Temple Scroll', *RQ* 15 (1991–92), pp. 543-67.
—'The Septuagint and the Temple Scroll: Shared "Halakhic" Variants', in G. Brooke and B. Lindars (eds.), *Septuagint, Scrolls and Cognate Writings: Papers Presented to the International Symposium on the Septuagint and its Relations to the Dead Sea Scrolls and Other Writings* (Atlanta, GA: Scholars Press, 1992), pp. 277-97.
—'The Temple Scroll in Literary and Philological Perspective', in W. Green (ed.), *Approaches to Ancient Judaism* (5 vols.; Chico, CA: Scholars Press, 1980), II, pp. 143-58.
H. Stegemann, 'The Literary Composition of the Temple Scroll and its Status at Qumran', in G. Brooke (ed.), *Temple Scroll Studies: Papers Presented at the International Symposium on the Temple Scroll, Manchester, December, 1987* (Sheffield: JSOT Press, 1989), pp. 123-48.
—'The Origins of the Temple Scroll', *VT* 40 (1988), pp. 235-56.
D. Swanson, 'The Use of the Chronicles in 11QT: Aspects of a Relationship', in D. Dimant and U. Rappaport (eds.), *The Dead Sea Scrolls: Forty Years of Research* (Leiden: E.J. Brill, 1992), pp. 290-98.

E. Tov, 'Deut. 12 and 11QTemple LII-LIII: A Contrastive Analysis', *RQ* 15 (1991), pp. 169-73.
—'The Temple Scroll and Old Testament Textual Criticism', *Eretz Israel* 16 (1982), pp. 100-111 (Hebrew).
M. Weinfeld, 'God versus Moses in the Temple Scroll—"I do not speak on my own but on God's authority" (Sifre Deut. sec. 5; John 12, 48f)', *RQ* 15 (1991–92), pp. 175-80.
A. Wilson and L. Wills, 'Literary Sources of the Temple Scroll', *HTR* 75 (1982), pp. 275-88.
M. Wise, 'Literary Criticism of the Temple Scroll (11QTemple)', *QC* 3 (1993), pp. 101-37.

Date and Provenance

M. Hengel, J. Charlesworth and D. Mendels, 'The Polemical Character of "On Kingship" in the Temple Scroll: An Attempt at Dating 11QTemple', *JJS* 37 (1986), pp. 28-38.
B. Levine, 'The Temple Scroll: Aspects of its Historical Provenance and Literary Character', *BASOR* 232 (1978), pp. 5-23.
L. Schiffman, 'The King, his Guard and the Royal Council in the Temple Scroll', *PAAJR* 54 (1987), pp. 237-59.
H. Stegemann, 'Is the Temple Scroll a Sixth Book of the Torah—Lost for 2500 Years?', in H. Shanks (ed.), *Understanding the Dead Sea Scrolls* (New York: Random House, 1992), pp. 126-36.
—'The Origins of the Temple Scroll', *VT* 40 (1988), pp. 235-56.

Purpose and Place in the Qumran Library

J. Baumgarten, 'Sadducean Elements in Qumran Law', in E. Ulrich and J. VanderKam (eds.), *The Community of the Renewed Covenant: The Notre Dame Symposium on the Dead Sea Scrolls* (Notre Dame: University of Notre Dame Press, 1994), pp. 27-36.
G. Brooke, 'The Temple Scroll: A Law unto Itself?', in B. Lindars (ed.), *Law and Religion: Essays on the Place of the Law in Israel and Early Christianity* (Cambridge: James Clarke, 1988), pp. 34-43, 164-66.
H. Burgmann, '11QT: The Sadducean Torah', in G. Brooke (ed.), *Temple Scroll Studies: Papers Presented at the International Symposium on the Temple Scroll, Manchester, December, 1987* (Sheffield: JSOT Press, 1989), pp. 257-63.
P. Callaway, 'The Temple Scroll and the Canonization of Jewish Law (11QTemple)', *RQ* 13 (1988), pp. 239-50.
H.-J. Fabry, 'Der Begriff "Tora" in der Tempelrolle', *RQ* 18 (1997), pp. 63-77.
D. Rokeah, 'The Temple Scroll, Philo, Josephus and the Talmud', *JTS* 34 (1983), pp. 515-26.
L. Schiffman, 'The Law of the Temple Scroll and its Provenance', *FO* 25 (1989), pp. 85-98.
—'Pharisaic and Sadducean Halakhah in Light of the Dead Sea Scrolls: The Case of Tevul Yom', *DSD* 1 (1994), pp. 285-99.
—'The Temple Scroll and the Nature of its Law: The Status of the Question', in E. Ulrich and J. VanderKam (eds.), *The Community of the Renewed Covenant: The Notre Dame Symposium on the Dead Sea Scrolls* (Notre Dame: University of Notre Dame Press, 1994), pp. 37-55.
—'The Temple Scroll and the Systems of Jewish Law of the Second Temple Period', in G. Brooke (ed.), *Temple Scroll Studies: Papers Presented at the International Symposium on the Temple Scroll, Manchester, December, 1987* (Sheffield: JSOT Press, 1989), pp. 239-55.
—'The Theology of the Temple Scroll', *JQR* 85 (1994), pp. 109-23.
H. Stegemann, 'Is the Temple Scroll a Sixth Book of the Torah—Lost for 2500 Years?', in H. Shanks (ed.), *Understanding the Dead Sea Scrolls* (New York: Random House, 1992), pp. 126-36.

J. VanderKam, 'The Theology of the Temple Scroll: A Response to Lawrence H. Schiffman', *JQR* 85 (1994), pp. 129-35.
M. Wise, 'The Eschatological Vision of the Temple Scroll', *JNES* 49 (1990), pp. 155-72.
Y. Yadin, 'Is the Temple Scroll a Sectarian Document?' in G. Tucker and D. Knight (eds.), *Humanizing America's Iconic Book: Society of Biblical Literature Centennial Addresses 1980* (Chico, CA: Scholars Press, 1982), pp. 153-69.

3

THE CONTENTS OF THE TEMPLE SCROLL

1. The Temple and its Courts

The plan for the Temple and its courts is a central concern of the Scroll, and prompted Yadin to name it 'The Temple Scroll'. As Yadin himself states,

> The most fascinating part of the scroll is perhaps the section devoted to the design and construction of the Temple, its rituals and procedures, and the sundry ordinances to safeguard the purity of the structure, the compound, and even the entire city in which it stood. This section takes up almost half the document, and because of its length and importance I have called the entire composition the Temple scroll (Yadin 1985: 112).

What was the impetus for this elaborate Temple plan, and what was the purpose?

The pseudepigraphical fiction of the Temple Scroll is that it was given directly by God to Moses on Mt Sinai. Thus, the plans for this Temple also came from God on Mt Sinai. There are two biblical clues to this situation. First, in Exod. 25.1-9 God commands Moses to build a sanctuary (*miqdāš*), 'in accordance with all that I show you concerning the pattern (*tabnît*) of the tabernacle and of all its furniture, so you shall make it' (Exod. 25.9). As we shall see, the description of the Tabernacle in Exodus 25 and the wilderness camp surrounding it (Num. 3–4) plays a crucial role in the plan of the Temple in the Temple Scroll. Second, in 1 Chron. 28.9-19, David gives to Solomon the plan of the Temple which he is to build, a plan which David claims was given to him by God: 'All this, in writing at the LORD's direction, he made clear to me the plan (*tabnît*) of all the works' (1 Chron. 28.19). Since, as I have shown above, the Temple Scroll is not creating *new* scripture, but is rather, through a process of careful exegesis of existing scripture, presenting what it claims as the correct interpretation of that scripture, the fact that God gave to Moses and David a pattern (*tabnît*) for God's sanctuary (*miqdāš*) means that an ideal plan exists and can be discovered and set out. It is likely (although not stated directly) that this Temple plan was meant to be the realization of the ideal pattern given to Moses and David. In fact, the author of this Temple plan draws heavily on all the descriptions of the sanctuary in the biblical text, especially Exodus 25–30 (the Tabernacle), 1 Kings 6 and 2 Chronicles 3–4 (Solomon's Temple), and Ezekiel 40–48 (the Temple of Ezekiel's vision). However, the author/redactor does not regard any of these Temple plans to be definitive or, evidently, divinely ordained; he uses elements of all of them to create what is a unique Temple plan found only in the Temple Scroll (Schiffman 1996: 570).

This Temple plan was not the creation of the author/redactor, however. The Temple plan is found in one of the sources of the Temple Scroll delineated by Wilson and Wills, cols. 2.1–13.8, 30.3–47.18 (Wilson and Wills 1982: 277). While I agree with their basic outline of the sources, I believe the so-called Temple Source began in column 3 rather than column 2, which is still part of the general introduction to the entire composition. Thus, the Temple Source would be found in cols. 3.1–13.8, 30.3–47.18. There is some evidence that this source existed apart from 11QTemple[a]. In 4Q365a, frags. 2, 3, 4 and 5 contain architectural details of the Temple and its courts. Some of this material overlaps with 11QTemple[a], but it is clearly not the same composition (White 1994: 317-33). Further, 4Q524, frag. 1, contains a small overlap with 11QTemple[a], col. 35.7 (Puech 1998: 90-91). As was discussed above, 4Q524 probably represents an earlier edition of the Temple Scroll. Thus, it is clear that the Temple plan in the Temple Scroll was not the creation of the author/redactor of 11QTemple[a], but comes from an earlier source. The source dates at least to the early second century BCE, and may be even earlier.

The goal of the plan for the Temple and its courts is to create a compound of concentric zones of holiness, in which the holiness emanating from the Divine Presence in the center, the Temple itself, radiates outward across the entire land of Israel. As the holiness radiates outward, so the levels of ritual purity progress inward, with each court demanding a higher degree of purity. The guiding architectural principle for this compound is the square (see the interesting work of Bean 1987, which is useful in outlining the architectural principles underlying the Temple plan). As the Scroll begins with the Temple itself and its furnishings, we will begin there as well.

3. *The Contents of the Temple Scroll*

a. The Temple

Columns 3–13, which contain the specifications for the Temple building, are unfortunately very fragmentary. However, by comparing the various biblical accounts to the preserved phrases of the Scroll, a basic understanding of what the Scroll is calling for can be obtained. Column 3 begins with the command to build the Temple and its furnishings: '... hou]se to put my name on it, a[ll ...' (col. 3.4). The Scroll then moves to specific details. Yadin (1983: II, 178-79) suggests that by giving the commands twice, once in a list and then in detail, the author/redactor is harmonizing the biblical accounts in Exodus 25-27 and 36-38. On the principle of moving from the inside outwards, the plan appears to begin with the furnishings of the Debir, the Holy of Holies, the innermost chamber of the Temple where the presence of God is to dwell.

The plan for the Debir and its furnishings is based on the Debir in the Tabernacle (Exod. 25.10-22; 26.31-33). The Tabernacle plan calls for a screened-off room within the Tabernacle proper, with a screen of blue, purple and crimson. Inside the Debir is the ark, a cover (*kappōret*), and two cherubim, all of which are to be covered with gold. This same configuration applied to Solomon's Temple, except that the cherubim were designed differently (1 Kgs 6.19-28).

The Scroll seems to call for the same configuration:

>] blue and purple [(col. 3.2)
> the] cover (*kappōret*) which is upon it, pure gold[... (col. 3.9)
> And two cherubim ... the end, the two spreading the wings[above the ark ... (col. 7.10-12)
> And you will make a gold curtain ... (col. 7.13)

The Scroll mentions some kind of curtain made of blue and purple, the ark, the gold cover for the ark, and two cherubim. The cherubim in the Scroll seem to conform to the design of the Tabernacle cherubim (Schiffman 1992a: 622, 625). The measurements of the Debir apparently are mentioned in col. 4.13, 'twenty cubits square', which corresponds to the measurements of the Debir in Solomon's Temple (1 Kgs 6.20).

The Scroll moves out from the Debir to the outer room of the sanctuary (the Heikhal; the word does not appear in cols. 3–13, but see col. 30.5). Here again the description of the Tabernacle, which calls for a table overlaid with gold for the Bread of the Presence and a gold lampstand with seven lamps, is the primary basis for the Scroll's reconstruction. The Scroll also calls for a Table for the Bread of the Presence:

> ... on the two rows[... th]is frankincense may go with the bread as a memorial portion ...] the incense altar, when [y]ou remove ...]bread, you shall put on it frankincense (col. 8.5-14)

and a menorah:] ... and [ ] flowers] from its two sides,] ... and on one side, three] ... and its hilt] ... three] the branch] three] and its snuffers, all (shall weigh) two talents (col. 9.1-14).

This is unlike Solomon's Temple, which had ten tables and ten menorahs (1 Chron. 4.7-8).

The description of the Temple itself resembles more closely the Temple of Solomon and Ezekiel's Temple, since it is a building rather than a tent shrine. The Temple has a main chamber, divided into the Debir and the Heikhal, a porch (*'ûlam*), and an 'upper room' above the Heikhal. It is surrounded by a cantilevered superstructure of six stories, a kind of reverse ziggurat. The measurements of the porch (ten cubits in depth, 60 cubits in height) are given (col. 4.9-10), but the other measurements are subject to conjecture.

b. The Inner Court

The plan of the Inner Court begins in col. 30. The Inner Court contains several buildings necessary for the functioning of the sacrificial cult. The first installation is a free-standing stairhouse, located on the northwest corner of the Heikhal (Yadin 1983: II, 131). The stairs of this stairhouse, which is similar to the stairhouse described in the New Jerusalem (see below, Chapter 4), climb around a central square pillar and give access to the roof of the Heikhal. The entire stairhouse, even the steps, are to be plated in gold.

The second installation mentioned is the House of the Laver, where the priests perform their ablutions after slaughter. The House of the Laver, with gates on the east, north and west, is to be located at the southeast corner of the Heikhal, diagonally opposite the stairhouse. It contains gold-plated niches for the priests to store their sacred vestments. The disposal of the washing water, which would become mixed with the blood of the sacrificial animals, is the subject of specific instructions. According to the Temple Scroll, the laver should contain a channel all around it, which will send the water down a drain and into the ground below the Inner Court; thus no one can use or touch it, since it is sacred (col. 32.12-15). This is in contrast to the practice of the Second Temple, in which, according to the Mishnah, the bloody water flowed into the brook Kidron and was used as manure in the Kidron valley (*m. Yom.* 5.6)! East of the House of the Laver is located the House of Utensils, the storage area for all the cultic paraphernalia. The House of Utensils has north and south gates and interior niches with doors as storage spaces.

Column 34 introduces a structure which may contain a clue to the dating of the Temple Source. It is an open-air slaughterhouse, consisting of 12 pillars supporting a roof. Its location is not preserved in the Temple

Scroll, but Yadin locates it in the southwest corner of the Inner Court (Yadin 1983: I, 206, fig. 5). Chains for securing the sacrificial animals dangled from the roof, and there was a mechanism utilizing wheels and rings for the slaughtering process itself. This mechanism appears to be similar, if not identical, to the one in use in the Second Temple from the time of John Hyrcanus:

> To the north of the Altar were rings, six rows of four each (and some say four rows of six each) at which they slaughtered the animal-offerings. The shambles lay north of the Altar, and there stood there eight short pillars; upon these were four-sided blocks of cedar-wood into which were fixed iron hooks, three rows to each, whereon they used to hang <the slaughtered beasts>. They used to flay them on marble tables between the pillars (*m. Mid.* 3.5 according to Yadin 1983: I, 230).

This mechanism, then, may provide an important clue to the dating of the Temple Source. If the Temple Source is merely imitating with approval an innovation already introduced in the Second Temple, then the date of the Temple Source must be after the beginning of the reign of John Hyrcanus, who introduced the innovation (thus post 135 BCE). This is the position of Hengel, Charlesworth and Mendels (1986: 37 n. 43). Alternatively, one can understand the Temple Source as advocating a system of slaughter that was subsequently adopted by Hyrcanus; this is the position adopted by Yadin (1985: 221-22), who also points out that Hyrcanus first followed the Pharisees in regard to cultic regulations, then switched to the Sadducees (Yadin 1985: 139-40). If Yadin is correct that the Temple Source is advocating the use of wheels in the Temple compound, it must be earlier than the reign of Hyrcanus (135 BCE). Further, if our argument above that the Temple Scroll reflects proto-Sadducean halakhah is correct, then Hyrcanus's introduction of the wheels may be the result of his shift to Sadducean practice. This would then accord with the date of the earlier edition of the Temple Scroll found in 4Q524, which is earlier than 150 BCE. The description of the House of Slaughter goes on to relate injunctions for flaying and butchering the sacrificial animals.

The next installation of the Inner Court mentioned in the Temple Source is a stoa of columns located to the west of, or behind, the Temple building. Its purpose seems to be for tethering the sacrificial animals; it is important that the sacrifices of the priests and the laity be kept separate:

> a stoa of standing columns for the sin offering and the guilt offering, separated from one another: for the sin offering of the priests and for the male goats and for the sin offerings of the people and for their guilt offerings, and all of them shall not be mixed one with another, for their places shall be separated from one another... (col. 35.10-13).

Bean (1987: 274), questions whether there is in fact a free-standing stoa behind the Temple; he prefers to understand the stoa as part of the Inner Court wall.

The final installation of the Inner Court, the sacrificial altar, is actually discussed in col. 12. Although col. 12 is very fragmentary, it seems to call for a stone altar with four horns, a bronze grill (col. 3), and a ledge (cols. 16 and 23). This description draws on elements from the altars of the Tabernacle, Solomon's Temple and Ezekiel's Temple (see Yadin 1983: I, 239-41). It is possible that the Temple and its out-buildings were meant to be surrounded by a low wall, similar to the one which surrounded the Second Temple as described by Josephus (*Ant.* 13.373; Yadin 1983: I, 205-207).

The Inner Court wall itself was to be square, measuring 280 cubits on each side (Yadin argues that this measurement is for the inner side [1983: I, 204], while Maier [1985: 63] argues that the measurements are given for the 'portico part' of the wall). The wall would have four gates, one on each side; these gates evidently were for the sons of Aaron (east), the sons of Kohath (south), the sons of Gershon (west), and the sons of Merari (north); in other words, the priests and the three levitical families. Although the names of these gates are not preserved in the Temple Scroll, they can be determined with a high degree of probability by noticing the apportionment of the chambers in the Outer Court to these clans (see below), and by comparing the location of these gates to the location of these clans in the wilderness camp (Num. 3.14-39) (Schiffman 1993b: 400). Since only ritually pure priests and Levites were allowed into the Inner Court, the names of the gates list those who were allowed through. The wall of the Inner Court contained a stoa with rooms for the priests and tables in front, kitchens for preparing the sacrifices on the sides of each gate, and stoves on each corner, all features necessary for the priests and Levites to cook and eat the sacrifices.

c. The Middle Court

The description of the Middle Court begins in col. 38. It is to be 480 cubits in length on each side, and 100 cubits wide. It is to have rooms 'in the wall on the outside' (col. 38.15). Yadin supposed that these rooms, like the rooms of the Inner Court, were to be made on the inner wall, facing into the Middle Court (see his reconstruction in 1985: 148), but Bean argues that 'on the outside' means that the rooms are to be constructed on the outer face of the wall, facing into the Outer Court (1987: 281). This would create an outside measurement of 500 cubits per side, the same as the court of Solomon's Temple, the outer court of Ezekiel's Temple, and the dimensions of the Temple Mount according to *m. Mid.* 2.1.

3. *The Contents of the Temple Scroll* 39

The Middle Court was restricted to ritually pure male Israelites over 20 years of age (col. 39.8-11). To accommodate them, the Middle Court has 12 gates, one for each of the sons of Jacob. The gates are arranged as follows: Simeon, Levi and Judah on the east (Levi is given pride of place, with Judah in the second position; this is in keeping with the Scroll's general tendency to favor the priests over the monarch); Reuben, Joseph and Benjamin on the south; Issachar, Zebulon and Gad on the west; and Dan, Naphtali and Asher on the north.

d. The Outer Court
The description of the Outer Court begins in col. 40. This third court is a major innovation of the Temple Scroll; none of the other Israelite Temples in antiquity, real or projected, had more than two courts. The purpose of this innovative third court is in keeping with the zones of holiness which the Scroll is establishing around the Temple; the Outer Court is for ritually pure Israelite women, children and proselytes, and allows them to participate in the public festivals of the Temple (see below), at a suitable remove.

As a consequence, the dimensions of the Outer Court are much greater than those of the Inner and Middle Courts. The Scroll calls for a measurement for each wall of 'about' 1600 cubits (col. 40.8). The approximateness of this measurement is striking, given that all the other measurements mentioned are exact. If exact measurements were given, one would arrive at either 1590 cubits or 1604 cubits (Yadin 1983: I, 251). Why, then, does the Scroll say 'about' 1600 cubits? Both Yadin and Bean attribute it to the author's predilection for round numbers (120, 480, 1600), while Bean also emphasizes the author's fondness for numbers that are multiples of 4, 7, 12, 50 and 360 (Yadin 1983: I, 254; Bean 1987: 290-91). In any case, the dimensions of the Outer Court are gigantic. As Broshi points out, 1600 cubits equals 2500 feet or half a mile. Thus, the total area of the Temple compound would be the same as the size of the entire city of Jerusalem in the second century BCE (Broshi 1992b: 115)!

The Outer Court will also have 12 gates, named after the sons of Jacob and exactly opposite the corresponding gates in the Middle Court: Simeon, Levi and Judah on the east; Reuben, Joseph and Benjamin on the south; Issachar, Zebulon and Gad on the west; and Dan, Naphtali and Asher on the north (cols. 40.14–41.11). This order of gates (and their measurements) appear nowhere else in the biblical and Second Temple literature,[1] with the exception of frag. 2 ii of 4Q365a (White 1994: 327-29).

---

1. The city gates (as much as they are preserved) in the New Jerusalem fragments have a very similar order; the gate of Simeon is on the northeast corner, and the gates

Since I have demonstrated that 4Q365a cannot be a precise copy of the Temple Scroll, this fragment may demonstrate that the Temple Source existed independently of the Temple Scroll (Crawford 1994: 259-73; see also Schiffman 1989a: 268), and preserves a unique tradition of Temple architecture.

The Outer Court is provided with installations to enable families and clans to celebrate the public festivals together. The outer wall has three stories (col. 42.10); each story has sets of rooms: an inner 'chamber', an outer 'room' and a porch as part of the stoa (cols. 41.17–42.9). On the roof of the outer wall are structures that are to be used to construct booths for the Festival of Sukkot (col. 42.10-17). All of the blocks of rooms between the gates are allocated to the various tribes and Levitical clans: on the east, on either side of the middle gate, the sons of Aaron are located. The sons of Aaron are given both pride of place and a double portion of rooms; Aaron thus symbolically receives the birthright among the Israelite clans in keeping with the Scroll's preference for the priests (Schiffman 1989a: 276). Simeon and Judah are also located on the east. On the south are located the tribes of Reuben, Joseph and Benjamin and the Levitical clan of Kohath; on the west the tribes of Issachar, Zebulon and Gad and the Levitical clan of Gershon; and on the north the tribes of Dan, Naphtali and Asher and the Levitical clan of Merari (see Yadin 1983: I, 267, fig. 23 for a helpful drawing of this layout). It is obvious from this arrangement that the Temple Source has a utopian vision of Israel as a worshipping community with the 12 tribes reunited in the land. For a reconstruction of the Temple and its three courts according to the plan of the Temple Scroll, see Figure 1.

e. Further Installations

The Temple Source ends with a description of several installations designed to guard even further the purity of the Temple. There are to be devices on the roofs of the walls (and possibly on the Temple itself) to prevent birds from befouling the Temple precincts (col. 46.1-4). Josephus and the Mishnah both describe devices ('scarecrows') to drive off birds from Herod's Temple (*War* 5.224; *m. Mid.* 4.6), while Eusebius, quoting Eupolemos, describes netting and bells that frighten away birds from Solomon's Temple (*Praep. Evang.* 451; for details see Yadin 1983: I, 271-72).

---

of Naphtali and Asher are on the north. The gates of Joseph and Reuben are also on the south, but in the New Jerusalem the gate of Joseph is on the southeast corner, while the gate of Reuben seems to be in the center or possibly on the southwest corner (4QNJar[a], frag. 1, cols.1–2). See also Wise 1990a: 78, although Wise thinks the gates of the Temple Scroll and the New Jerusalem are in exactly the same order.

3. *The Contents of the Temple Scroll*

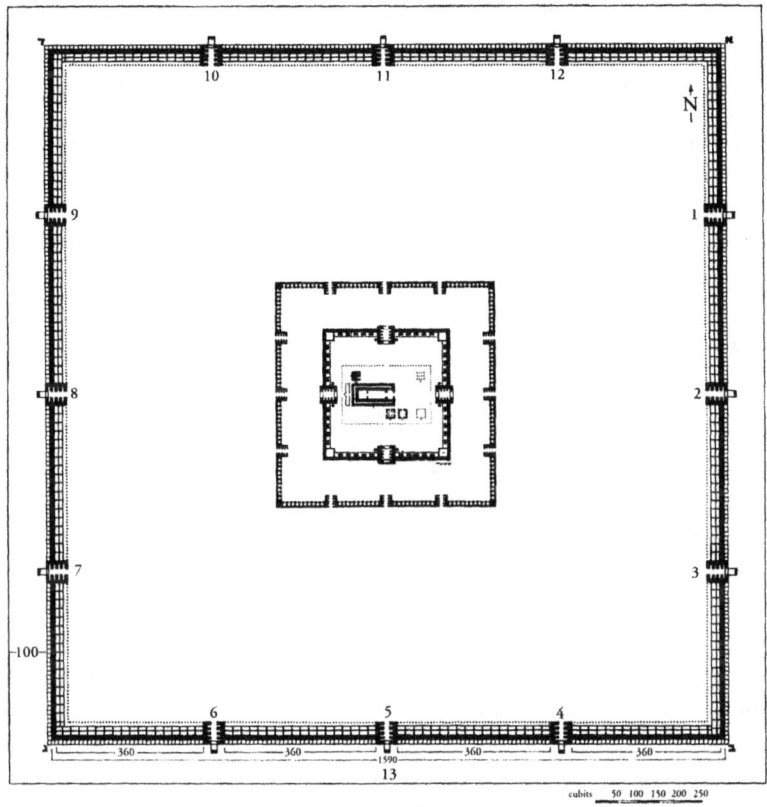

Figure 1. The Temple and its three courts. Illustration from Yigael Yadin, *The Temple Scroll* (Jerusalem: Israel Exploration Society, 1983), I, p. 252.

Around the Outer Court there is to be a terrace (רובד) 14 cubits wide, with 12 steps leading up to it. Yadin suggests that this terrace is to be built at each of the gate entrances (Yadin 1983: I, 273), while Bean argues that a continuous terrace around the entire outer wall is meant (1987: 288). Outside the terrace a fosse (חיל) is to be constructed, to 'separate the holy Temple from the city so that they do not suddenly enter my Temple and defile it' (col. 46.9-11). It is not clear whether the fosse is a moat or a mound, but that it functions as a barrier is clear. Latrines are to be installed 3000 cubits to the north-east of the temenos, which are to be roofed structures with pits. This piece of information, which seems to indicate that the author of the Temple Source viewed defecation as ritually defiling, is one of the clues that Yadin used to propose Essene (and Qumranic) authorship for the Temple Scroll (Yadin 1985: 179-82). Josephus states that the Essenes had unusual toilet habits and viewed defecation as defiling (*War* 2.147-49); the War Scroll (usually considered a Qumran sectarian document) places the latrine at a distance of 2000 cubits from the war camp so that 'no immodest nakedness shall be seen in the surroundings of all their camps (War Scroll, col. 7.7). Finally, de Vaux uncovered in the excavations at Qumran an installation which has been identified by J. Magness as a latrine (Magness 1998b: 37-40). This latrine conforms to the specifications of the Temple Scroll, since it is a roofed structure with a pit. All this is convincing evidence that the Temple Scroll is at the least related to the Qumran sectarian movement.

Finally, to the east of the city, three areas are to be set apart for those defiled by leprosy, gonorrhea and nocturnal emission. These categories of persons may not enter the city until they have been properly purified. These are the last structures mentioned in the Temple Source. It is interesting to note that the Temple Scroll does not appear to envision, or at least discuss, a city surrounding the Temple complex, as we shall see is the focus of concern for the New Jerusalem. The lack of mention of a city will be important in the discussion of the purity regulations below. The entire plan of the Temple, as outlined above, presents a scheme in which holiness radiates outward from a central core. The aim of the Temple Scroll is to protect that holiness with purity regulations that grow increasingly stringent as one progresses inward. This brings us to the second major topic to be considered, the purity regulations.

2. The Purity Regulations

Wilson and Wills (1982: 280) suggest that cols. 48–51.10 can be isolated as a separate source, which they entitle 'Purity Laws'. They note that these columns use the second person plural address throughout, along with several divine third person references. Column 51.5b-10, which changes to a first person divine referent and uses both second person singular and plural addresses, they consider a redactional seam (Wilson and Wills 1982: 281). Callaway questions whether a separate purity source can be isolated, and argues instead for a coherent purity 'section', which begins in col. 45 and ends with col. 51.10 (Callaway 1985–87: 221). Swanson, on the other hand, concludes that cols. 48–51 were originally independent of cols. 45–47 and constitute a separate Purity Law. Further, he suggests that col. 47 serves as a redactional bridge from laws pertaining to the Temple or Temple City to other purity regulations (Swanson 1995: 184). Wise, however, in the most plausible reconstruction, notes that the hand of the redactor is very evident in the purity laws, and suggests that the author/redactor of the Temple Scroll did not have a text of a so-called 'Purity Law' in front of him, but rather drew on one or more existing collections of purity regulations, which he used by interlarding the regulations for the purity of the Temple City into the end of the Temple Source (as well as using portions of these collections elsewhere in the Scroll) and then creating a block of purity regulations in cols. 47–51, with col. 47 serving as a redactional bridge as Swanson has suggested (Wise 1990a: 133-34).

Many studies have been done concerning the nature of the purity regulations in the Temple Scroll (see especially the articles of Baumgarten, Milgrom and Schiffman listed at the end of the chapter, as well as the comments of Yadin 1983: I). The purity regulations as found in the Pentateuch are chiefly concerned with maintaining the purity of the wilderness camp and the people of Israel. Yadin, basing himself on the work of G. Alon, argues that in the Second Temple period there were two basic positions regarding the application of those purity laws: a minimalist position, which limits the laws of purity to the area of the Temple and its priests, and a maximalist position, which extends the laws of purity to all of Israel (Yadin 1983: I, 277). Milgrom agrees that there is a distinction to be made, but asserts that it stems from two different sources within the Pentateuch, P (the Priestly source) and H (the Holiness Code). P posits a contiguous community with a sanctuary at its center. 'Any impurity, incurred anywhere in the community... will pollute the sanctuary.' H, on the other hand, posits the holiness of the land, independent of the Temple (Milgrom 1989: 167). P thus takes a minimalist position: the sacred sphere is limited to the Tabernacle and its surrounding encampment, while H takes the maximalist view: the sacred sphere is coextensive with the land (Milgrom 1989: 167). Both Yadin and Milgrom agree that the author/redactor of the Temple Scroll (and his sources) is a maximalist, extending the purity regulations to cover the widest sphere. In order to investigate this maximalist position in the Temple Scroll, I will concentrate on the laws concerning women.[2]

I have already mentioned (p. 42) that the purity laws strive to protect the holiness of the Temple by growing increasingly stringent as one moves geographically closer to the Temple. Thus, the 'everyday' purity regulations found in the Temple Scroll concern women's lives in the ordinary cities of Israel, with special legislation for the City of the Sanctuary. The Temple Scroll applies the regulations of the Levitical camp in the wilder-

---

2. As Schiffman has noted, 'the Qumran materials do not demonstrate a systemic approach to issues concerning women,' and their views concerning women are 'extremely conservative' (Schiffman 1992b: 210 n. 2, 228). Nevertheless, since laws concerning women are most often concerned with the major purity areas of sexuality and bodily discharge, they form a good focus for our study.

ness to the cities of Israel; thus all cities were to be maintained in a state of Levitical purity (Schiffman 1990a: 138). Therefore there were to be places set aside in every city for women who were menstruating or had just given birth: 'And in every city you shall allot places for... women during their menstrual uncleanness and after giving birth, so that they may not defile in their midst with their menstrual uncleanness' (col. 48.16, 18). This regulation is based on Lev. 12.2-8, the laws concerning a parturient, and Lev. 15.19-30, which gives the laws of menstruation and irregular blood flows. Both of these passages imply that during her period of impurity a woman is excluded from the Levitical camp. Since in the Scroll such women are excluded from all cities (the subject relative to the City of the Sanctuary will be discussed below), these regulations represent a significant intensification of the concept of the impurity of female body functions (Japhet 1993: 78 and Himmelfarb 1999: 17).

Columns 49–51 contain an extensive section listing the regulations concerning corpse impurity, in which the laws pertaining to the wilderness camp are extended to all cities, and regulations concerning a dead body in a tent are extended to a house (Num. 19.10-15). The general thrust of these regulations is to extend the biblical prescription, mainly by analogy; for example, while the Torah calls for a person who has had contact with the dead to purify themselves with water on the third and seventh days (Num. 19.12, which calls for sprinkling on the third day and sprinkling, bathing and laundering on the seventh), the Scroll calls for purification with water on the *first*, third and seventh days. The extra day (which requires bathing and laundering) seems to come from the laws concerning a person made impure by touching the carcass of an unclean animal (Lev. 11.24-25), the person afflicted with a skin disease (Lev. 14.8-9), or a man with a genital discharge (Lev. 15.5-11), all of whom must immerse themselves on the first day (see further Yadin 1983: I, 331-33; Schiffman 1990a: 146-47; Milgrom 1978b: 512-18; Milgrom cites a parallel with 1QM 14.2-3). These regulations, extensive as they are, indicate a particular halakhic position; one in particular, the rule concerning a pregnant woman whose fetus dies in the womb, is certainly controversial.

> And if a woman is pregnant, and her child dies in her womb, all the days on which it is dead inside her, she is unclean like a grave; and every house she comes into is unclean, with all its furnishings, for seven days. And anyone who touches it shall be unclean until the evening; and if he enters the house with her, he shall be unclean seven days. And he shall wash his clothes and bathe himself on the first day; and on the third day he shall sprinkle and wash his clothes and bathe himself; and on the seventh day he shall sprinkle for the second time and wash his clothes and bathe himself, and at the going down of the sun he will become clean (col. 50.10-16).

According to this regulation, a woman carrying a dead fetus conveys impurity in the same way that a grave does; she renders a house impure just like a dead body; one who enters her house must be purified as for a dead body; and the furnishings of the house must likewise be purified. This legislation has no direct biblical basis at all. However, we find this question a subject of controversy among the rabbis: the majority of the sages, in an anonymous ruling, stated that a dead fetus does not convey impurity (to its mother or anyone else) until it leaves the womb (*m. Ḥul.* 4.3) because the womb makes the fetus a 'swallowed impurity'. However, according to *b. Ḥul.* 72a Rabbi Akiva held that a dead fetus did impart impurity, even in its mother's womb. The argument is one of analogy, with the text in question being Num. 19.16: 'Whoever in the open field touches one who has been killed by a sword, or who has died naturally, or a human bone, or a grave, shall be unclean seven days'. Graves convey uncleanness; therefore if one accidentally encounters one ('in an open field'), certain purification procedures must be adhered to. The Scroll further protects against this possibility by setting aside designated areas for cemeteries, one for every four cities (col. 48.11-14). But is encountering a woman carrying a dead fetus like encountering a grave 'in an open field?' According to the Temple Scroll, the answer is 'yes'; according to the later rabbis, 'no'. The appearance of this legislation in the Temple Scroll shows that this controversy dates back at least to the second century BCE.

The regulations discussed above concern women living in the ordinary cities. The regulations concerning the Temple City have the effect of making it very difficult for women to reside, even temporarily, in the Temple City. I have already mentioned in the discussion of the Temple courts that women were prohibited from entering the Middle Court of the Temple (col. 39.7-9). There are several other regulations pertaining to the sanctity of the Temple that affect women. The most striking of these is found in col. 45.11-12, concerning sexual intercourse: 'And if a man lies with his wife and has an emission of semen, he shall not come into any part of the city of the temple, where I will settle my name, for three days'. The difficulty is not the sexual intercourse itself, but the ejaculation of semen, as can be seen by the preceding regulation: 'And if a man has a nocturnal emission, he shall not enter into any part of the temple until he will complete three days' (col. 45.7-8). While a man may have a nocturnal emission when he is alone, sexual intercourse (in the world view of the Scroll) occurs only with one's wife. Thus women are affected, and sexual intercourse is effectively banned from the Temple City. This inferred ban on sexual intercourse is clearly spelled out in the Damascus Document: 'No man should sleep with his wife in the city of the temple, defiling the city of the temple with their impurity' (CD 12.1-2). The ban, and the three-day period of purification associated with it, is based on Exod. 19.10-15:

> the LORD said to Moses: 'Go to the people and consecrate them today and tomorrow. Have them wash their clothes and prepare for the third day, because on the third day the LORD will come down upon Mount Sinai in the sight of all the people. You shall set limits for the people all around, saying, 'Be careful not to go up the mountain or touch the edge of it. Any who touch the mountain shall be put to death. No hand shall touch them, but they shall be stoned or shot with arrows, whether animal or human being, they shall not live'. When the trumpet sounds a long blast, they may go up on the mountain'. So Moses went down from the mountain to the people. He consecrated the people, and they washed their clothes. And he said to the people, 'Prepare for the third day; *do not go near a woman*' (emphasis mine).

The Pentateuch texts specifically concerned with the emission of semen, Lev. 15.16-18 and Deut. 23.10-12, prescribe a one-day period of purification, where only a single immersion is required and the man remains in the camp. In the Temple Scroll the impurity lasts three days, requires two immersions and two launderings, and the man is entirely removed from the Temple City. Milgrom suggests that the Scroll's concept of purity is layered, and therefore requires more elaborate rituals to effect two transitions: the first from impurity to the common, and the second from the common to the holy (Milgrom 1991: 162). It is also evident from col. 45.9 (and cols. 49.20; 50.4, 16; 51.3) that the Temple Scroll would reject the Pharisaic and Rabbinic concept of טבול יום (*ṭĕvûl yôm*), by which an impure person who had undergone immersion was considered 'partially' clean; according to the Scroll, those who had undergone the purification rituals, including immersion, still remained totally impure until sundown: 'and when the sun is down, he may come within the temple' (col. 45.10; this was first remarked on by Yadin 1983: I, 332; see also Baumgarten 1994: 29 and Schiffman 1989d: 247, who notes that this agrees with 4QMMT as well). The regulation (and the purification rituals associated with it) in the Temple Scroll and the Damascus Document thus equates the Temple, where God's presence dwells, with Sinai, where God descended to give the Torah to the Israelites.

This same understanding of the sanctity of the holy things is found in 1 Sam. 21.4-6, where the priest Ahimelek refuses to give the Bread of the Presence to David and his men unless they have 'kept themselves from women'. It may also be present in 2 Chron. 8.11, where Solomon builds a separate house for his wife, Pharaoh's daughter, because 'my wife shall not live in the house of King David of Israel, for the places to which the ark of the LORD has come are holy'. Japhet notes that all three of these passages 'illustrate the general idea of opposition between sanctity (the holiness of the holy place and of the shewbread) on the one hand, and sexual relations on the other hand. This contrast is presented with respect not to the priests but to everyone in Israel' (Japhet 1993: 79). The Temple Scroll certainly adopts this idea.

Yadin uses the ban on sexual intercourse in the Temple City to argue that women were banned from permanent residence in the Temple City and in this enforced celibacy on the part of the men is found the roots of Essene celibacy (Yadin 1983: I, 289). Yadin's logic is faulty on several counts. First, the ban on sexual intercourse would apply only to married women, not to unmarried, widowed or divorced women (see also Japhet 1993: 72). There would be no reason these latter classes of women would be prohibited from residing in the Temple City. Second, simply because sexual intercourse was banned in the Temple City does not mean that married couples could not reside there, at least for short periods (such as festivals); they simply could not engage in sexual intercourse during that period. Third, it is increasingly clear that the Qumran sect (which Yadin identified with the Essenes) was not ideologically celibate, although they were certainly conservative in their views on sexuality.

However, Yadin's question of the *permanent* residence of women in the Temple City is certainly valid, and several more pieces of evidence in the purity regulations may provide an answer. As noted above, col. 46 states that three areas outside the Temple compound are to be set aside where those who have had a nocturnal emission, those who suffer from skin disease and gonorrheacs can be quarantined. These are based on the regulations concerning the wilderness camp in Num. 5.2-3: 'Command the Israelites to put out of the camp everyone who is leprous, or has a discharge, and everyone who is unclean through contact with a corpse; you shall put out both male and female, putting them outside the camp; they must not defile their camp, where I dwell among them.' What is missing is a place for those defiled by corpse uncleanness (Num. 5.2); they are simply denied entry until purifications (col. 45.17). Also, women during menstruation and after childbirth (Lev. 12.2-5 and 15.19-31, where such women are by implication banned from the Tabernacle) are not allotted quarantine areas. However, according to the Temple Scroll quarantine areas for menstruants and parturients are to be set aside in the other cities of Israel (see above). Further, there are elaborate regulations concerned with corpse uncleanness, in which it is explicitly stated, 'and when a man dies in your cities' (col. 49.5). These regulations include purification rituals for the house in which the person has died (col. 49.5-21), after which 'by evening they will become clean of the dead, to touch all their pure stuff'. Clearly, the author/redactor of the Temple Scroll has strong views concerning female impurity (*niddah*) and corpse impurity, but he does not apply them to the Temple City. Why not?

The answer may lie in the answer to the difficult question of the definition of the phrase '*îr hammiqdāš* ('city of the sanctuary'), which appears in col. 45.11-12, in the regulation concerning sexual intercourse. Yadin assumes that the '*îr hammiqdāš* is the equivalent of the entire holy city (Yadin 1983: I, 288-89). Indeed, as noted above, the dimensions of the Temple compound described in the Temple Scroll did encompass the entire area of the city of Jerusalem in the second century BCE (it is important to note that the name 'Jerusalem' does not appear in the Temple Scroll, thus preserving the pseudepigraphical setting on Mt Sinai). Yadin likewise assumes that the same phrase in CD 12.1-2 also means the entire city of Jerusalem, as first proposed (but rejected) by Ginzberg (1976: 73-74). B. Levine criticized this definition, suggesting instead that '*îr hammiqdāš* was a designation for the Temple compound rather than the entire city. Levine argued that it was impractical to forbid intercourse within the city or to locate toilets outside the city, but there was no difficulty if these regulations only applied to the Temple compound (Levine 1978: 14-17).

Milgrom and Schiffman have carried on the debate, with Milgrom following Yadin and Schiffman following Levine. Schiffman argues in several articles that '*îr hammiqdāš* refers only to the Temple compound or the temenos, based on the understanding that the Scroll does not make a distinction between the terms *hammiqdāš* ('sanctuary') and '*îr hammiqdāš* (Schiffman 1986: 307; see also 1993b: 403-405). Schiffman also argues, along the same lines as Levine, that the fact that menstruants and parturients 'lived in the various cities but did not live in the city of the sanctuary, [is] a strong argument for considering the '*îr hammiqdāš* to be only the sacred precincts. It is difficult to imagine that the entire city of Jerusalem was to be free of women and celibate' (Schiffman 1986: 313). He does note, however, that the Scroll does not give any details concerning the 'hinterland' beyond the Temple City (Schiffman 1993b: 403).

Milgrom, on the contrary, argues that 'the construct עיר המקדש can only mean: the עיר that contains the מקדש. If עיר were limited to the sacred compound, then המקדש would have to be the Temple building', which is contrary to normal usage, in which it designated the Temple and its precincts (Milgrom 1994: 126). Thus, according to the Temple Scroll, God's presence would dwell on all Jerusalem rather than just the Temple compound, which Milgrom terms 'a major innovation of the Scroll' (1994: 127; see also Wacholder 1983: 225).

A reconciliation may be possible between these two views. First, it should be noticed that the Scroll is silent on the subject of dwellings and/or tribal allotments beyond the fosse mentioned in col. 46. This is in marked contrast to the Temple plan of Ezekiel, who envisions the priests living in houses around the sanctuary (Ezek. 45.3-4), and the New Jerusalem, which preserves an extensive city plan (see Chapter 4). It is also in obvious contrast to the historical Temples, which had extensive residential districts surrounding them. Second, the Scroll makes no provision for the realities of everyday life for Jerusalem. There are not, as mentioned, quarantine areas for menstruants and parturients, as there are for other cities; those contracting corpse impurity are banned from entry. The Temple Scroll decrees that there are to be separate cemeteries throughout Israel, one for every four cities (col. 48.11-14), but no mention is made of a cemetery for Jerusalem. Further, the only vessels of animal skin allowed in the 'city of my temple' are those made from animals sacrificed in the temple (col. 52.13-16). In other words, the city wherein lies the Temple is not like other cities; in fact, it is forbidden for other cities to be like the Temple City: 'you shall not purify any city among your cities like my city' (col. 47.14-15). The city of the Temple is unique because God dwells there: 'The city which I will hallow by settling my name and [my] temp[le within it] shall be holy and clean of any unclean thing with which they may be defiled; everything that is in it shall be clean' (col. 47.3-6). Therefore, I would argue that the Temple City is not envisioned by the author/redactor of the Temple Scroll as having permanent residents, but as a place of *temporary* residents. The Israelites will come to the Temple from their cities for festivals and various rites, and then return to their cities. The priests would come in their particular course. Thus, menstruating and parturient women, or those who have had contact with the dead would simply not come to the city (on the subject of menstruants and parturients, see also Milgrom 1978a: 26). Sexual intercourse would be banned during the period of temporary residence. However, those who discovered a skin disease, gonorrhea or had a nocturnal emission during their temporary residence would have to be put outside in the quarantine areas. Thus Yadin is partially correct; women were banned from permanent residence in the city, but so was everyone else. The only permanent resident of the City of the Temple is God.

3. The Festival Calendar

Of all the sources for the Temple Scroll posited by Wilson and Wills, there is near unanimous agreement that the Festival Calendar, cols. 13.9–30.2, is a separate piece that may once have circulated independently (Wilson and Wills 1982: 279; Wise 1990a: 129). The Festival Calendar was inserted by the author/redactor of the Temple Scroll into the Temple Source, after the description of the altar (cols. 12.8–13.7; 13.8 contains a blank line) and before the description of the Stairhouse in the Inner Court. The purpose of the Festival Calendar is to outline the sacrifices and the rituals of the various festivals held in the Temple (hence its placement after the description of the altar). The biblical base text of the Festival Calendar is Numbers 28–29, itself a festival calendar, along with the extensive use of Leviticus 23 and other texts as appropriate.

Column 13.10-16, which is very fragmentary, appears to contain the commands for the daily burnt offering, or *tāmîd* (Exod. 29.38-42; Num. 28.3-8). As with each type of animal for burnt offering which follows, the Festival Calendar specifies the cereal and drink offerings to be given with the animal, sometimes (although not in this case) departing from the biblical base text in order to do so. After the daily offerings come the commands for the Sabbath offering (cols. 13.17–14.02), based on Num. 28.9-10. The commands for the Sabbath offering are followed by commands for the New Moon (or first of the month) offerings (col. 14.2-8; Num. 28.11-15; 15.1-13). Thus the Festival Calendar completes the ordinary sacrificial schedule before moving on to the ordinances for the great yearly festivals.

The first annual festival is the New Moon of the first month, the Spring New Year (cols. 14.9–15.2). The base text is Num. 29.1-6, although the Numbers passage is discussing the first day of the seventh month (the Fall New Year); the author of the Festival Calendar applies the commands for the Fall New Year to the Spring New Year by analogy. The Spring New Year held special significance for the author of the Temple Scroll; it was the day on which the construction of the Tabernacle took place (Exod. 40.2); also, according to the book of *Jubilees*, Jacob arrived at Bethel on the eve of the first day of the first month (*Jub.* 29.19; cf. col. 29.10). Labor is prohibited, and the sacrifices are enumerated. The disposition of the sin offering is of particular interest. The goat for the sin offering is to be offered *first*, and the sin offering is accompanied by cereal and drink offerings, contrary to rabbinic ruling (*m. Men.* 9.6; Yadin 1983: I, 143-47; Schiffman 1995a: 46-47; Milgrom 1993b: 100-101).

The next annual festival is one of the striking innovations of the Temple Scroll. The Scroll calls for an annual festival for the ordination of priests, in order to formalize the reappointment of all the priests for the coming year (col. 15.3-10). As Schiffman notes, there is no biblical basis for any annual priestly appointment rituals (Schiffman 1994a: 255); in Exodus 29 and Leviticus 8 the ceremony for the ordination of Aaron and his sons by Moses is described, but the ceremony is never repeated. According to the Scroll, the ordination is to be celebrated annually, on the first seven days of Nisan; special rites are called for in the case of the ordination of a new

3. *The Contents of the Temple Scroll*

High Priest. In the place of Moses the elders of the priests (זקני הכוהנים) are to perform the elevation ceremony (Lev. 8.26-29).

Following the commands concerning the ordination festival come the commands concerning the great pilgrimage festival of Passover (col. 17.6-16; Exod. 12.1-13; Lev. 23.5; Num. 9.2-5; Deut. 16.5-7). The Festival Calendar takes its cue from Deuteronomy; the Passover is to be celebrated in the Temple; it is not a household celebration (Deut. 16.5-7; cf. 2 Kgs 23.21-23; 2 Chron 30.13; 35.1). The Passover sacrifice must be offered before the evening *tāmîd*, contrary to rabbinic ruling (*m. Pes.* 5.1). It must be eaten only by those aged 20 and above; this conclusion is arrived at by analogy with Exod. 30.14 and Num. 1.2-3. While no time limit other than 'by morning' is put on the eating of the lamb, it must be eaten within the Temple precincts (the Karaites agreed with this ruling, while the rabbis contended that it could be eaten anywhere in Jerusalem). The feast of Unleavened Bread begins on the fifteenth day of Nisan and lasts for seven days (Lev. 23.6-8). The Scroll's ordinances concerning the Passover celebration and the Feast of Unleavened Bread agree with those of *Jubilees* (*Jub.* 49).

The next group of festivals contains another major innovation of the Festival Calendar. While the biblical text calls for only one festival of First Fruits, that of grain (the Feast of Weeks, Num. 28.26-31; Lev. 23.15-21), the Festival Calendar calls for four First Fruits festivals, a festival of barley (col. 18.1-10), of wheat (cols. 18.10–19.9), of wine (cols. 19.11–21.10), and of oil (cols. 21.12–23.2). The latter two festivals also appear in other texts discovered in the caves surrounding Qumran (4QMMT, 4Q327, 4Q409 [reconstructed]).

These four festivals are to be celebrated at 50-day intervals from each other, beginning with barley in the spring and ending with oil in the fall, times which coincide with the produce harvests. The first festival, the First Fruits of Barley, begins immediately after the Feast of Unleavened Bread. In the biblical text this is not a full-fledged first fruits festival, but is the day of the Omer (the 'waving of the sheaf'; Lev. 23.10-14). However, by the Second Temple period the connection between the Omer celebration and barley was well-established (Yadin 1983: I, 102). The second first fruits festival, that of wheat, is found in the biblical text at Lev. 23.15-21 and Num. 28.26-31. The author uses these biblical passages to reconstruct the offerings for the non-biblical first fruits festivals. The First Fruits of Wheat is to be held 50 days after the First Fruits of Barley; the method of counting called for gives us the greatest insight into the calendar envisioned by the Temple Scroll.

Yadin interpreted the data of the Temple Scroll to claim that the Scroll used the solar calendar of 364 days espoused by *1 Enoch*, *Jubilees* and the

Qumran community. The interval between each first fruits festival is reckoned as follows:

> And you shall count seven full sabbaths from the day that you brought the sheaf of the wave offering; you shall count to the morrow after the seventh sabbath, counting [fifty] days (col. 18.10-13).

> [And] you shall count from the day that you brought the new cereal offering to the Lor[d,] [th]e bread of new fruits, seven weeks; seven full sabbaths [there shall be] until you count fifty days to the morrow of the seventh sabbath (col 19.11-13).

> And y[ou sha]ll count from that day on seven weeks seven times, nine and forty days, seven full sabbaths there shall be, until the morrow of the seventh sabbath you shall count fifty days (col. 21.12-14).

These reckonings are based on Lev. 23.15-17:

> And from the day after the sabbath, from the day on which you bring the sheaf of the elevation offering, you shall count off seven weeks; they shall be complete. You shall count until the day after the seventh sabbath, fifty days...[3]

According to the Festival Calendar, there should be 148 days from the Feast of Barley to the Feast of Oil. Yadin argued that the word 'sabbath' in the Festival Calendar always means 'Saturday' (as against the rabbis, who understood 'sabbath' as the last day of the festival), so that the counting always began on a Sunday. This reflects an ancient controversy concerning how to understand 'the day after the sabbath' in Lev. 23.15-16. The Pharisees understood it to mean 'the day after the end of the festival', based on the following phrase 'from the day on which you bring the sheaf of the elevation offering', and counted accordingly. The Sadducees (and Samaritans, Boethusians and Karaites) understood it to mean the Sabbath that fell *during* the festival; thus their Feast of Weeks would have begun earlier than that of the Pharisees. Now it seems that the Temple Scroll (along with the book of *Jubilees*) offers a third alternative; the counting should begin on the Sunday after the Sabbath which falls after the end of the festival (Milgrom 1984: 128).

Yadin also noticed that the first day of each cycle was counted twice, since it was also the last day of the previous cycle; thus 'fifty days' and 'seven weeks' denoted the same length of time. Finally, he argued that, based on a fragment of 4QCalendrical Document E^b (4Q327), the Feast of Oil fell on the twenty-second of Ellul. If one counts the weeks accord-

---

3. It will be noticed that the Temple Scroll lacks the phrase 'from the day after the sabbath' in col. 19.11-13; it is difficult to determine whether or not the phrase was missing from the base text or deliberately omitted in the Festival Calendar to make the system of reckoning more clear.

3. The Contents of the Temple Scroll   53

ing to the solar calendar, starting the Sunday after the Sabbath which follows the end of the barley festival, one would arrive at the twenty-second of Ellul for the Feast of Oil (Yadin 1983: I, 116-22). However, Yadin's reasoning was circular; it did not prove that the Temple Scroll presumed the solar calendar, but only that the reckoning of the Temple Scroll was *compatible* with the solar calendar (Levine 1978: 10; Stegemann 1992b: 169-76). The publication of 4QMMT throws new light on the subject: 4QMMT A begins with a calendar which is clearly a 364-day solar calendar (l. 20), and whose reckoning of the Feast of Weeks and the festivals of New Wheat, New Wine and New Oil correspond to the reckoning of the Temple Scroll (Glessmer 1999: 271). Thus, it appears almost certain that the Temple Scroll did appropriate the 364-day solar calendar, and used it in the fixing of its Festival Calendar.

As stated above, the new first fruits festivals of wine and oil were celebrated by the Qumran community, even though they are not mentioned in the Torah. However, the formula 'the grain, the wine and the oil', which occurs throughout biblical literature (Num. 18.12; Deut. 7.13, 11.14, 12.17, 14.23, 18.4, 28.51; 2 Kgs 18.32; Hos. 2.10, 24 *et al.*) may have given rise to the notion that these festivals were meant to be celebrated. Further, Num. 18.12 mandates that the new wine and new oil are to be tithed, and 2 Chron. 31.5 mentions that the people tithed wine and oil during the reign of Hezekiah. Among the Qumran texts the Feast of Oil is mentioned in 4QCalendrical Document E[b], 4QReworked Pentateuch[c], and 4QMMT A.

The celebrations of these first fruit festivals was tied to the practice of tithing, as is shown in col. 43.4-17:

> On these days it shall be eaten; and let [them] not leave of it from one year to another year. For thus they shall eat it: from the feast of the first fruits of the grain of wheat they shall eat the grain to the following year, until the feast of the first fruits; and the wine, from the day of the feast of wine, until the day of the feast of the wine of the following year; and the oil, from the day of its feast to the following year, until the feast, the day of offering of new oil on the altar. And all that remains of their feasts shall be consecrated and burnt; it shall never again be eaten, for it is holy. And those who dwell at a distance of a three-days' journey from the temple shall bring whatever they can bring. And if they cannot carry it, let them sell it for money and bring the money and buy with it grain, wine and oil and cattle and sheep; and they shall eat it on the days of the feasts. But they shall not eat of it on the working days in their sorrows, for it is holy. But on the holy days it shall be eaten, and it shall not be eaten on the working days…

Here the Scroll is discussing the tithe commanded in Deut. 14.22-26:

> Set apart a tithe of all the yield of your seed that is brought in yearly from the field. In the presence of the LORD your God, in the place that he will choose

> as a dwelling for his name, you shall eat the tithe of your grain, your wine, and your oil, as well as the firstlings of your herd and flock, so that you may learn to fear the LORD your God always. But if, when the LORD your God has blessed you, the distance is so great that you are unable to transport it, because the place where the LORD your God will choose to set his name is too far away from you, then you may turn it into money. With the money secure in hand, go to the place that the LORD your God will choose; spend the money for whatever you wish—oxen, sheep, wine, strong drink, or whatever you desire. And you shall eat there in the presence of the LORD your God, you and your household rejoicing together.

This tithe is given and eaten in connection with the harvest. As Baumgarten has demonstrated, the Scroll's discussion of the tithe contains several unique features: there was a one-year limit on the consumption of the tithe and, because it was holy, it could only be eaten on feast days, not ordinary days. The tithe can be sold for money, which is then brought to the Temple and used to buy produce to consume there, but it is not redeemed for money. All of these regulations may be polemical, since they are contrary to later rabbinic practice, which did not allow selling the tithe (Baumgarten 1985: 12-13).

Immediately following the Festival of Oil is yet another new festival, the Wood Festival (col. 23.1–25.1). There is no basis in the Torah for this festival; however, in Neh. 10.34 it is related that certain families were selected by lot to bring wood to the Temple at certain times of the year. This wood offering bears little resemblance to the Wood Festival found in the Temple Scroll. The latter is a six-day festival with multiple offerings, during which two tribes per day presented their wood offering. The tribal order is unique; it is different from the tribal order of the gates of the Middle and Outer Courts, thus strengthening the argument for two different sources. In the Wood Festival, Levi and Judah again take pride of place, with Levi receiving preference over Judah. The biblical basis for this festival is obscure, unless a clue can be found in the manuscript 4QReworked Pentateuch[c].

4QReworked Pentateuch[c] (4QRP[c], 4Q365) is a manuscript of the Torah characterized by numerous exegetical additions and reworkings. Its date of composition is unknown; its paleographic date falls between 125 and 75 BCE (Tov and White 1994: 255-318). Fragment 23 of 4QRP[c] runs as follows:

> in booths you shall dwell seven days, every citizen in Israel shall dwell in booths, in order that your generations may know that I caused your fathers to dwell in booths when I brought them out from Egypt; I am the LORD your God.
>
> And Moses declared the festivals of the LORD to the children of Israel. And the LORD spoke to Moses saying, Command the children of Israel saying,

3. *The Contents of the Temple Scroll*   55

> When you come to the land which I am giving to you for an inheritance, and you dwell upon it securely, you will bring wood for a burnt offering and for all the wo[r]k of [the h]ouse which you will build for me in the land, to arrange it upon the altar of burnt offering, and the calv[es] for the passover sacrifices and for whole burnt offerings and for thank offerings and for freewill offerings and for burnt offerings, daily ... and for the doors and for all the work of the house the[y] will br[ing ...] the [fe]stival of fresh oil. They will bring wood two [by two]; the ones who bring on the fir[st] day, Levi [... Reu]ben and Simeon and [on t]he fou[rth] day ...

For a complete discussion of this fragment, see Tov and White 1994: 290-96. The fragment begins with a quotation of Lev. 23.24–24.2, then continues with an exegetical addition in which God gives Moses commands for further celebrations. The Feast of Oil is mentioned in l. 9, followed immediately by commands for bringing wood to the Temple. It is evidently to be brought on six consecutive days, with two tribes bringing the wood each day (ll. 9-11). These lines are parallel with the Wood Festival in the Temple Scroll; in fact, Yadin used this fragment to help him reconstruct the Temple Scroll (Yadin 1983: III, supplementary plates, pl. 40*, 1). It is possible that this fragment (and 4QRP^c as a whole) served as a souce for the Festival Calendar or the Temple Scroll as a whole (Stegemann 1988: 237, 253; see also Wise 1990a: 49, who suggests it is part of his 'D source').

The Festival Calendar continues with regulations for the Fall New Year, the first day of the seventh month, proclaimed with a trumpet blast (col. 25.2-10; Lev. 23.23-25; Num. 29.1-6). The offering of the morning *tāmîd* and the New Moon offering are followed by the special offerings for the Fall New Year, which are identical with those of the Spring New Year.

The tenth of the seventh month brings the Day of Atonement (cols. 25.10-27.10; Lev. 23.26-32; Num. 29.7-11; Lev. 16.2-34). The day calls for self affliction, although the Scroll does not specify what that means; it is probable that it signified fasting, as in current practice.

The last festival mentioned in the Festival Calendar is the Feast of Sukkôt, or Booths (cols. 27.10–29.1; Num. 29.13–30.1; Lev. 23.33-36). The festival, which begins on the fifteenth day of the seventh month, lasts for seven days; on the eighth there is a final solemn convocation. Although the command to dwell in booths is lost, it probably appeared at the bottom of col. 27. As we noted in the section on the Temple and its Courts, permanent frames for constructing booths were to be erected on the top of the wall of the Outer Court (col. 42.10-17). These booths are to be used by designated officials to fulfill the custom of sitting in booths in the Temple precincts during the sacrifice (Neh. 8.16; Schiffman 1985: 230).

It is worth noting that the Festival Calendar does not include the celebrations of Hannukah and Purim; Hannukah did not exist, and Purim may not have existed, at the time when the Festival Calendar was written. It is unlikely that they would have been accepted by the author/redactor of the Temple Scroll or the Qumran community.

One of the striking features of the regulations for the sacrificial cult in the Temple Scroll is that the Levites are accorded a higher status than in the Pentateuch. They are given tribal status in the architecture of the Temple compound, both in the gates of the middle and outer courts and the assignment of chambers in the outer court (cols. 39–40, 44). They are also listed first among the tribes for the wood offering (cols. 23–24). This tribal status has no biblical precedent. In col. 22, the Levites are to perform the sacrifice ('the sons of Levi shall slaughter'); this opposed the practice of the Second Temple (Milgrom 1978b: 502). The Levites are given the following perquisites from the cult: during the New Wine and New Oil festivals, they receive one pair of the 14 lambs and 14 rams (col. 22.12); they also receive the first tithe of the harvest festivals, one one hundredth of the spoils of war and of the hunt, one tenth of the wild honey, and one fiftieth of the wild doves (col. 60.6-9; Milgrom 1978b: 502). These tithes are based on Num. 18.21-24 and Lev. 27.30. Further, the Levites receive the shoulder (שכם) of the peace offerings (cols. 21.02-05; 22.8-11; 60.6-7), a perquisite that is again without biblical precedent (Milgrom 1983: 169-76). Finally, the Levites are given certain judicial functions: judges are chosen from the Levites as well as the priests (col. 61.8-9; cf. Deut. 19.17) and the Levites are represented, along with the priests and the Israelites, on the king's cabinet (col. 57.12-15). This higher status for the Levites in the Temple Scroll is probably an influence from Ezekiel 43–44, and is echoed in *Jubilees* and the Damascus Document (see Chapter 5). It reflects the ideology of the levitical and priestly circles which produced the Temple Scroll.

The final lines of the Festival Calendar (col. 29.2-10), which incorporate material from several biblical passages, summarize the author's intention:

> These [you shall offer to the Lord at your appointed feasts ...] for your burnt offerings and for your drink offerings [...] in the house upon which I shall [settle] my name [...] burnt offerings, [each] on its [proper] day, according to the law of this ordinance, continually from the children of Israel, besides their freewill offerings for all their offerings, for all their drink offerings and all their gifts which they will bring to me that th[ey] may be accepted. And I will accept them, and they shall be my people, and I will be theirs for ever, [and] I will dwell with them for ever and ever. And I will consecrate my [t]emple by my glory, on which I will settle my glory, until the day of creation [Yadin: blessing] on which I will create my temple and establish it for

myself for all times, according to the covenant which I have made with Jacob at Bethel.

The festivals are to be celebrated perpetually, in the Temple where God's glory dwells, until God builds his own Temple on 'the day of creation'. This second temple is clearly an eschatological temple; thus the temple of the Temple Scroll, although ideal, is meant to be an earthly temple built by human hands (Yadin 1983: I, 182-87; II, 129, see also Swanson 1994: 175; contra Wacholder 1983: 21-30 and Wise 1990b: 158). The significance of the 'covenant which I have made with Jacob at Bethel' is obscure; we have already noted that Jacob first arrived at Bethel, according to *Jubilees*, on the first day of the first month; also according to *Jubilees*, Levi was appointed to his eternal priesthood at Bethel on the festival of Sukkôt (*Jub.* 31–32). Further, in *Jubilees* 31–32 God promises, as part of his covenant with Jacob, to build an eternal sanctuary. If the Temple Scroll is referring to this promise here, it must be drawing on the same tradition as *Jubilees*.

4. The Deuteronomic Paraphrase and the Law of the King

The final section of the Temple Scroll (cols. 51.11-66) is best described as a Deuteronomic paraphrase; the book of Deuteronomy serves as the base text, and it even follows the essential order of Deuteronomy 12–26. Wilson and Wills discerned two separate sources in this material, the 'Laws of Polity' (cols. 51.11–56.21 and 60.1–66.17) and the 'Law of the King' (cols. 57–59; Wilson and Wills 1982: 281-83). Schiffman basically agrees with this division, but suggests that the Law of the King was a pre-existent source, and that the Laws of Polity material, better termed the Deuteronomic Paraphrase, was composed by the author/redactor of the Temple Scroll himself for the Scroll (Schiffman 1991–92a: 545, 567). Wise, on the other hand, argues for two different sources, a 'Deuteronomy Source' (cols. 2.1-15; 48.1-10a; 51.11-18; 52.1-12; 53.1–56.21; 60.12–63.14a; 64.1-6a; 64.13b–66.9b; 66.10-12a), which is not the book of Deuteronomy but a collection of laws drawn from Deuteronomy, and a 'Midrash to Deuteronomy' source (cols. 56.1–59.21; 60.2-11; and 64.6b-13a), which may have been 'a political treatise formulated by means of interpolative scriptural exegesis' (Wise 1990a: 35, 38, 101, 110). Wise's extension of the Deuteronomic Paraphrase to include material prior to col. 51 seems without merit; in col. 2, for example, the base text is Exodus 34, with reference to Deuteronomy 7. It is difficult to determine when the Deuteronomic Paraphrase was composed (see further on the question of date above), but the Law of the King does appear to be a separate source which may have circulated independently before its inclusion in the Deuteronomic Paraphrase; we will discuss the Law of the King first.

a. The Law of the King

The Law of the King (cols. 57–59) is an outgrowth or continuation of the biblical 'Law of the King' (Deut. 17.14-20), which appears in col. 56.12-21. The redactor's use of Deut. 17.14-20 gives some useful insights into the Scroll's attitude to the office of kingship. It takes the office of kingship for granted; this is in keeping with the Scroll's ideal view of Israel: united in the land as 12 tribes, with a temple and priesthood at its center and a king as secular head of the government (this is similar to the ideals of the Deuteronomistic History and the Chronicler's History). The text of Deuteronomy used by the redactor of the Deuteronomic Paraphrase contains several variants from the MT text of Deuteronomy, some of which are certainly deliberate. One example will suffice: Deut. 17.16 reads 'Only he must not multiply for himself horses (TS סוס; MT סוסים), and he must not cause the people to return to Egypt *for war* in order to multiply *for himself* horses *and silver and gold*, as *I have said* to you (TS לכה; MT לכם), "you shall not return (TS sing.; MT pl.) on this (TS feminine; MT masculine) road again".' The most noticeable change is the change from third person to first person, which we have come to expect from the Temple Scroll. It is attributable to the author/redactor of the Scroll in the service of his divine fiction. Verse 16 displays a major variant from the ancient witnesses; for 'to Egypt' (מצרימה) it reads 'to Egypt for war' (מצרים למלחמה). Yadin calls this a 'halakhic explanation' (1983: I, 80); indeed, it changes the nature of the passage by prohibiting war (and plunder) but evidently, through silence, permitting trade and other peaceful activities. This is an example of the insertion of an exegetical comment directly into a verse.[4] A series of similar small exegetical changes in the text of Deuteronomy introduce the redactor's view of the role and position of the king, a striking feature of which is the king's subordination to the priesthood; this view is considerably enlarged and strengthened in the 'Law of the King' which follows.

---

4. At the end of v. 16, the Temple Scroll adds 'and silver and gold' (וכסף וזהב), not an exegetical variant but an anticipation of the phrase in 17.17. Wise 1990a: 113-14, argues that למלחמה was added to the text after the addition of וכסף וזהב. Thus he argues that למלחמה is exegetically insignificant. While I agree with his argument that למלחמה is not helpful for dating the passage, the presence of the word still points to *exegetical* activity within the text of Deuteronomy; further, since no other ancient witnesses contain למלחמה, it is impossible to argue convincingly that it was *not* added by the redactor.

3. *The Contents of the Temple Scroll*

Column 57 begins with 'And this is the law ...', surely referring back to 56.21 (Deut. 14.18). According to 1 Sam. 10.25, Samuel wrote down all the rights and duties of kingship and 'laid it up before the LORD'. However, according to the Temple Scroll, 'this law' was given by God on Sinai, and so precedes the actual institution of kingship by several centuries. The Law proceeds topically, drawing freely on all parts of the canonical biblical text for its halakhic conclusions, including the only use of Song of Songs in the Temple Scroll (Song 3.8; col. 59.9-11). This extensive use of biblical material taken from outside of the Torah is unique to the Law of the King (Wise 1990a: 106).

The topics covered in the Law are:

1. The muster of the army (57.1-5).
2. The king's guard (57.5-11).
3. The royal council (57.11-15).
4. The queen (57.15-19).
5. Prohibition against corruption (57.19-21).
6. Laws of war (58.3-21).
7. Curse and blessing (59.2-21).

I shall use as an example of the statutes of the Law of the King the regulations concerning the queen (col. 57.15-19):

> And he shall not take a wife from all the daughters of the nations, but from his father's house he shall take unto himself a wife, from the family of his father. And he shall not take upon her another wife, for she alone shall be with him all the days of her life. But should she die, he may take unto himself another from the house of his father, from his family.

The regulations concerning the king's marriage impose certain limits that did not apply to any biblical king: the king must marry a Jewish woman; the woman must be from his own clan and family; the king may not take a second wife while the first one is alive, but he may remarry if he becomes a widower. The regulations clearly presuppose the biblical prohibitions of marriage with non-Jews (Exod. 34.16; Deut. 7.3-7), which by the early Second Temple period had become a source of conflict within the Jewish community (Ezra 9–10; Neh. 13.23-29; cf. the book of Esther, with its absence of polemic against marriage to a Gentile). The rule that the king must marry within his own clan and family uses language from Gen. 24.37-38 (Abraham's instructions concerning Isaac's marriage) and Num. 36.6-8 (the daughters of Zelophehad). Yadin (1983: I, 355) understands the rule as imposing the marriage law of the high priest (Lev. 21.14) on the king, but it may also be understood to mean that the king may not marry a proselyte, but only a blood Israelite (Schiffman 1992b: 215).

The next regulation, a ban on polygamy and possibly divorce, is intriguing. Polygamy, the taking of more than one wife, is clearly banned. The language of the Scroll echoes Lev. 18.18: 'And you shall not take a woman as a rival to her sister, uncovering her nakedness while her sister is still alive'. If the term 'sister' is understood as 'any fellow woman' (so the Karaites), then polygamy is forbidden. As Yadin and others have noted, the Damascus Document also polemicizes against polygamy and probably divorce: '… are caught twice in fornication: by taking two wives in their lifetime' (CD 4.20-21; for a discussion of this passage in light of the Temple Scroll, see Hempel 2000).

The prohibition on divorce is oblique, but implied by the phrase 'she alone shall be with him all the days of her life'. If the Temple Scroll is indeed banning divorce, it is in conflict with Deut. 24.1-4, which permits divorce and remarriage. Other passages in the Temple Scroll seem to assume that divorce is permitted, in fact, taken for granted; for example, col. 54.4-5 declares that the vow of a divorced woman holds good. Can the contradiction be resolved? Yadin understood the ban on polygamy and divorce found in this regulation to apply to all Israelites (Yadin 1985: 201); however, the Law of the King is only referring to the king, and other passages in the Scroll countenance divorce; it therefore seems safer to interpret the ban as applying only to the king.

b. The Deuteronomic Paraphrase

The Deuteronomic Paraphrase exhibits the same techniques of scriptural exegesis I have noted elsewhere in the Scroll, this time consistently using Deuteronomy as the base text. It functions as a collection of laws for life in the land. I will investigate two controversial regulations from the collection: the rule concerning execution by hanging (col. 64.6-13) and the incest prohibitions (col. 66.12-17).

The passage concerning execution by hanging reads as follows:

> If a man informs against his people, and delivers his people up to a foreign nation, and does harm to his people, you shall hang him on the tree, and he shall die. On the evidence of two witnesses and on the evidence of three witnesses he shall be put to death, and they shall hang him on the tree. And if a man has committed a crime punishable by death, and defected into the midst of the nations, and has cursed his people the children of Israel, you shall hang him also on the tree, and he shall die. And their body shall not remain upon the tree all night, but you shall bury them on the same day, for those hanged on the tree are accursed by God and men; you shall not defile the land which I give you for an inheritance.

The biblical base text is Deut. 21.22-23:

3. *The Contents of the Temple Scroll*

> When someone is convicted of a crime punishable by death and is executed, and you hang him on a tree, his corpse must not remain all night upon the tree; you shall bury him that same day, for anyone hung on a tree is under God's curse. You must not defile the land that the LORD your God is giving you for possession.

Several differences are immediately noticeable. The Deuteronomic Paraphrase specifies the nature of the crimes 'punishable by death'; they are political crimes against the nation. There is no biblical basis for this understanding, although historically the practice was common (cf. Est. 7.9-10). Second, the word order of MT, 'is executed and you hang him on a tree' (והומת ותלית אתו על עץ) is reversed in the Temple Scroll: 'you shall hang him on the tree, and he shall die' (ותליתמה אותו על העץ וימת). Thus hanging becomes the method of execution, and not exposure after death. The verb תלה might refer to impalement, hanging or crucifixion, although crucifixion was a common method of political execution in the late Second Temple period (Baumgarten 1972: 476). Yadin (1983: I, 374-79) understands the use of תלה in the Temple Scroll to refer to crucifixion, and sees it as a deliberate exegetical change on the part of the author/redactor as part of an ongoing controversy with the Pharisees, who opposed capital punishment by crucifixion. However, Wise has demonstrated that the reversed word order may already have been present in the author/redactor's base text (Wise 1990a: 122). In any case, the text of the Temple Scroll sheds interesting light on one understanding of capital punishment in the Second Temple period.

The prohibitions against incest occur in col. 66.11-17:[5]

> A man shall not take his father's wife, nor shall he uncover his father's skirt. A man shall not take his brother's wife, nor shall he uncover his brother's skirt, be it his father's son or his mother's son, for this is impurity. A man shall not take his sister, his father's daughter or his mother's daughter, for this is an abomination. A man shall not take his father's sister or his mother's sister, for it is wickedness. A man shall not take his brother's daughter or his sister's daughter, for it is an abomination. A [man] shall not take ...

The Deuteronomy base text is 23.1, 'a man shall not marry his father's wife, thereby violating his father's rights', but the prohibitions scattered throughout the biblical text are gathered together here: for the brother's wife, Lev. 18.16, 20.21; for the sister, Lev. 20.17 and Deut. 27.22; for the aunt, Lev. 18.12-14. The prohibition against marriage to a niece is not biblical, but is the result of exegesis: if it is forbidden for a man to marry

---

5. In 4Q524, frags. 15-22, the prohibitions against incest continue for several lines after the end of col. 66 in 11QTemple[a], thereby demonstrating that the Temple Scroll existed in more than one recension. See Puech 1998: 103-108.

his aunt (Lev. 18.12-14), it is equally forbidden for a woman to marry her uncle. The Samaritans, early Christians, Falashas and Karaites all prohibited uncle-niece marriage, as did evidently the sect at Qumran. The Damascus Document polemicizes against it:

> And each man takes as a wife the daughter of his brother and the daughter of his sister. But Moses said: 'Do not approach your mother's sister, she is a blood relation of your mother'. The law of incest, written for males, applies equally to females, and therefore to the daughter of a brother who uncovers the nakedness of the brother of her father, for he is a blood relation (CD 5.7-11).

The Deuteronomic Paraphrase gives a series of regulations concerning life in the land of Israel. By placing this section at the end of the composition, the author/redactor thus continues the pattern begun in his description of the Temple and its courts; the Scroll moves from the most holy (the Temple and its rituals) to the less holy (ordinary life in the land).

Further Reading

General Studies
F. García Martínez, 'The Temple Scroll and the New Jerusalem', in P. Flint and J. VanderKam (eds.), *The Dead Sea Scrolls after Fifty Years* (2 vols.; Leiden: E.J. Brill, 1999), II, pp. 431-60.
J. Maier, *The Temple Scroll: An Introduction, Translation, and Commentary* (trans. R.T. White; Sheffield: JSOT Press, 1985).
J. Milgrom, 'The Temple Scroll', *BA* 41 (1978), pp. 105-20.
H. Stegemann, 'The Institutions of Israel in the Temple Scroll', in D. Dimant and U. Rappaport (eds.), *The Dead Sea Scrolls: Forty Years of Research* (Leiden: E.J. Brill, 1992), pp. 156-85.
D. Swanson, *The Temple Scroll and the Bible: The Methodology of 11QT* (Leiden: E.J. Brill, 1995).
B.Z. Wacholder, *The Dawn of Qumran: The Sectarian Torah and the Teacher of Righteousness* (Cincinnati, OH: Hebrew Union College Press, 1983).
A. Wilson and L. Wills, 'Literary Sources of the Temple Scroll', *HTR* 75 (1982), pp. 275-88.
M. Wise, *A Critical Study of the Temple Scroll from Qumran Cave 11* (SAOC, 49; Chicago: Oriental Institute of the University of Chicago, 1990).
Y. Yadin, *The Temple Scroll* (3 vols.; Jerusalem: Israel Exploration Society, 1983).

The Temple and its Courts
P. Bean, 'A Theoretical Construct for the Temple of the Temple Scroll' (Master's Thesis; Eugene, OR: University of Oregon, 1987).
B. Bokser, 'Approaching Sacred Space', *HTR* 78 (1985), pp. 279-99.
G. Brooke, 'The Temple Scroll and the Archaeology of Qumran, 'Ain Feshka and Masada' (11QTemple)', *RQ* 13 (1988), pp. 225-37.
M. Broshi, 'The Gigantic Dimensions of the Visionary Temple in the Temple Scroll', in H. Shanks (ed.), *Understanding the Dead Sea Scrolls* (New York: Random House, 1992), pp. 113-15.
M. Delcor, 'Is the Temple Scroll a Source of the Herodian Temple?', in G. Brooke (ed.),

3. The Contents of the Temple Scroll 63

Temple Scroll Studies: Papers Presented at the International Symposium on the Temple Scroll, Manchester, December, 1987 (Sheffield: JSOT Press, 1989), pp. 67-89.

S. Japhet, 'The Prohibition of the Habitation of Women: The Temple Scroll's Attitude toward Sexual Impurity and its Biblical Precedents', *JANES* 22 (1993), pp. 69-87.

B. Levine, 'The Temple Scroll: Aspects of its Historical Provenance and Literary Character', *BASOR* 232 (1978), pp. 5-23.

J. Maier, 'The Architectural History of the Temple in Jerusalem in the Light of the Temple Scroll', in G. Brooke (ed.), *Temple Scroll Studies: Papers Presented at the International Symposium on the Temple Scroll, Manchester, December, 1987* (Sheffield: JSOT Press, 1989), pp. 23-62.

J. Milgrom, 'The City of the Temple', *JQR* 83 (1994), pp. 125-28.

—' "Sabbath" and "Temple City" in the Temple Scroll', *BASOR* 232 (1978), pp. 25-27.

—'Studies in the Temple Scroll', *JBL* 97 (1978), pp. 501-23.

L. Schiffman, 'Architecture and Law: The Temple and its Courtyards in the Temple Scroll', in J. Neusner, E. Frerichs and N. Sarna (eds.), *From Ancient Israel to Modern Judaism: Intellect in Quest of Understanding. Essays in Honor of Marvin Fox* (4 vols.; Atlanta, GA: Scholars Press, 1989), II, pp. 267-84.

—'The Construction of the Temple According to the Temple Scroll', *RQ* 17 (1996), pp. 555-71.

—'The Furnishings of the Temple According to the Temple Scroll', in J. Trebolle Barrera and L. Vegas Montaner (eds.), *The Madrid Qumran Congress: Proceedings of the International Congress on the Dead Sea Scrolls, Madrid, 18–21 March 1991* (Leiden: E.J. Brill, 1992), pp. 621-34.

—'The House of the Laver in the Temple Scroll', *Eretz Israel* 26 (1999), pp. 169-75.

—'Sacred Space: The Land of Israel in the Temple Scroll', in A. Biran and J. Aviram (eds.), *Biblical Archaeology Today: Proceedings of the Second International Congress on Biblical Archaeology 1990* (Jerusalem: Israel Exploration Society, 1993), pp. 398-410.

The Purity Regulations

G. Brin, *Studies in Biblical Law: From the Hebrew Bible to the Dead Sea Scrolls* (trans. J. Chapman; Sheffield: JSOT Press, 1994).

P. Callaway, 'Source Criticism of the Temple Scroll: The Purity Laws', *RQ* 12 (1985–87), pp. 213-22.

M. Himmelfarb, 'Sexual Relations and Purity in the Temple Scroll and the Book of Jubilees', *DSD* 6 (1999), pp. 11-36.

S. Japhet, 'The Prohibition of the Habitation of Women: The Temple Scroll's Attitude toward Sexual Impurity and its Biblical Precedents', *JANES* 22 (1993), pp. 69-87.

B. Levine, 'The Temple Scroll: Aspects of its Historical Provenance and Literary Character', *BASOR* 232 (1978), pp. 5-23.

J. Milgrom, 'The Concept of Impurity in Jubilees and the Temple Scroll', *RQ* 16 (1993), pp. 277-84.

—'Deviations from Scripture in the Purity Laws of the Temple Scroll', in S. Talmon (ed.), *Jewish Civilization in the Hellenistic-Roman Period* (Sheffield: JSOT Press, 1991), pp. 159-67.

—'First Day Ablutions in Qumran', in J. Trebolle Barrera and L. Vegas Montaner (eds.), *The Madrid Qumran Congress: Proceedings of the International Congress on the Dead Sea Scrolls, Madrid, 18–21 March 1991* (Leiden: E.J. Brill, 1992), pp. 561-70.

—'The Qumran Cult: Its Exegetical Principles', in G. Brooke (ed.), *Temple Scroll Studies: Papers Presented at the International Symposium on the Temple Scroll, Manchester, December, 1987* (Sheffield: JSOT Press, 1989), pp. 165-80.

L. Schiffman, 'Exclusion from the Sanctuary and the City of the Sanctuary in the Temple

Scroll', in R. Ahroni (ed.), *Biblical and Other Studies in Memory of Shelomo D. Goitein* (Columbus, OH: Ohio State University Press, 1986), pp. 301-20.

—'The Impurity of the Dead in the Temple Scroll', in *idem.* (ed.), *Archaeology and History in the Dead Sea Scrolls: The New York University Conference in Memory of Yigael Yadin* (Sheffield: JSOT Press, 1990), pp. 135-57.

—'Laws Pertaining to Women in the Temple Scroll', in D. Dimant and U. Rappaport (eds.), *The Dead Sea Scrolls: Forty Years of Research* (Leiden: E.J. Brill, 1992), pp. 210-28.

—'The Prohibition of the Skins of Animals in the Temple Scroll and Miqsat Ma'ase Hatorah', *WCJS* 10 (1990), pp. 191-98.

E. Schuller, 'Women in the Dead Sea Scrolls', in M. Wise (ed.), *Methods of Investigation of the Dead Sea Scrolls and the Khirbet Qumran Site: Present Realities and Future Prospects* (New York: Academy of Sciences, 1994), pp. 115-31.

The Festival Calendar

G. Anderson, 'The Interpretation of the Purification Offering (החטאת) in the Temple Scroll (11QTemple) and Rabbinic Literature', *JBL* 111 (1992), pp. 17-35.

J. Baumgarten, 'The First and Second Tithes in the Temple Scroll', in A. Kort and S. Morschauer (eds.), *Biblical and Related Studies Presented to Samuel Iwry* (Winona Lake, IN: Eisenbrauns, 1985), pp. 5-15.

R. Beckwith, 'The Temple Scroll and its Calendar: Their Character and Purpose', *RQ* 18 (1997), pp. 3-19.

G. Brin, *Studies in Biblical Law: From the Hebrew Bible to the Dead Sea Scrolls* (trans. J. Chapman; Sheffield: JSOT Press, 1994).

G. Brooke, 'The Feast of New Wine and the Question of Fasting', *ET* 95 (1984), pp. 175-76.

—'The Temple Scroll—A Law unto Itself?' in B. Lindars (ed.), *Law and Religion: Essays on the Place of the Law in Israel and Early Christianity* (Cambridge: James Clarke, 1988), pp. 34-43, 164-66.

S. Crawford, 'Three Fragments from Qumran Cave 4 and their Relationship to the Temple Scroll', *JQR* 85 (1994), pp. 259-73.

M. Delcor, 'La fête des huttes dans le Rouleau du Temple et dans le Livre des Jubilés', *RQ* 15 (1991), pp. 181-98.

B. Levine, 'A Further Look at the Mo'adim of the Temple Scroll', in L. Schiffman (ed.), *Archaeology and History in the Dead Sea Scrolls: The New York University Conference in Memory of Yigael Yadin* (Sheffield: JSOT Press, 1990), pp. 53-66.

—'The Temple Scroll: Aspects of its Historical Provenance and Literary Character', *BASOR* 232 (1978), pp. 5-23.

J. Milgrom, 'New Temple Festivals in the Temple Scroll', in T. Madsen (ed.), *The Temple in Antiquity: Ancient Records and Modern Perspectives* (Provo, UT: Brigham Young University Press, 1984), pp. 125-33.

—'On the Purification Offering in the Temple Scroll', *RQ* 16 (1993), pp. 99-101.

—'The Qumran Cult: Its Exegetical Principles', in G. Brooke (ed.), *Temple Scroll Studies: Papers Presented at the International Symposium on the Temple Scroll, Manchester, December, 1987* (Sheffield: JSOT Press, 1989), pp. 165-80.

—'Qumran's Biblical Hermeneutics: The Case of the Wood Offering', *RQ* 16 (1993–94), pp. 449-56.

—' "Sabbath" and "Temple City" in the Temple Scroll', *BASOR* 232 (1978), pp. 25-27.

—'The Shoulder for the Levites', in Y. Yadin, *The Temple Scroll* (rev. edn; Jerusalem: Israel Exploration Society, 1983), pp. 169-76.

—'Studies in the Temple Scroll', *JBL* 97 (1978), pp. 501-23.

3. The Contents of the Temple Scroll

L. Schiffman, ' 'ôlâ and ḥaṭṭā't in the Temple Scroll', in D. Wright (ed.), *Pomegranates and Golden Bells: Studies in Biblical, Jewish and Near Eastern Ritual, Law, and Literature in Honor of Jacob Milgrom* (Winona Lake, IN: Eisenbrauns, 1995), pp. 39-48.

—'The Millû'îm Ceremony in the Temple Scroll', in G. Brooke and F. García Martínez (eds.), *New Qumran Texts and Studies: Proceedings of the First Meeting of the International Organization for Qumran Studies Paris 1992* (Leiden: E.J. Brill, 1994), pp. 255-73.

—'Sacral and Non-Sacral Slaughter According to the Temple Scroll', in D. Dimant and L. Schiffman (eds.), *Time to Prepare the Way in the Wilderness: Papers on the Qumran Scrolls* (Leiden: E.J. Brill, 1995), pp. 69-84.

—'The Sacrificial System of the Temple Scroll and the Book of Jubilees', in Kent Harold Richards (ed.), *SBL Seminar Papers*, 24 (Chico, CA: Scholars Press, 1985), pp. 217-33.

—'Shelamim Sacrifices in the Temple Scroll', *Eretz Israel* 10 (1989), pp. 176-83.

A. Shemesh, ' "Three-Days' Journey from the Temple": The Use of this Expression in the Temple Scroll', *DSD* 6 (1999), pp. 126-38.

H. Stegemann, 'The Institutions of Israel in the Temple Scroll', in D. Dimant, U. Rappaport (eds.), *The Dead Sea Scrolls: Forty Years of Research* (Leiden: E.J. Brill, 1992), pp. 156-85.

D. Swanson, ' "A Covenant Just Like Jacob's": The Covenant of 11QT 29 and Jeremiah's New Covenant', in G. Brooke and F. García Martínez (eds.), *New Qumran Texts and Studies: Proceedings of the First Meeting of the International Organization for Qumran Studies Paris 1992* (Leiden: E.J. Brill, 1994), pp. 273-86.

M. Wise, 'The Covenant of the Temple Scroll XXIX, 3-10', *RQ* 14 (1989), pp. 49-60.

—'A New Manuscript Join in the "Festival of Wood Offering" (Temple Scroll XXIII)', *JNES* 47 (1988), pp. 113-21.

The Deuteronomic Paraphrase and the Law of the King

J. Baumgarten, 'Does TLH in the Temple Scroll Refer to Crucifixion?', *JBL* 91 (1972), pp. 472-81.

M. Bernstein, 'Midrash Halakhah at Qumran? 11QTemple 64:6-13 and Deuteronomy 21:22-23', *Gesher* 7 (1979), pp. 145-66.

G. Brin, 'Divorce at Qumran', in M. Bernstein, F. García Martínez, J. Kampen (eds.), *Legal Texts and Legal Issues: Proceedings of the Second Meeting of the International Organization for Qumran Studies, Cambridge 1995. Published in Honour of J.M. Baumgarten* (STDJ, 23; Leiden: E.J. Brill, 1997), pp. 231-44.

M. Delcor, 'Le statut du roi d'après le Rouleau du Temple', *Henoch* 3 (1981), pp. 47-68.

M. Hengel, J. Charlesworth and D. Mendels, 'The Polemical Character of "On Kingship" in the Temple Scroll: An Attempt at Dating 11QTemple', *JJS* 37 (1986), pp. 28-38.

D. Mendels, ' "On Kingship" in the Temple Scroll and the Ideological Vorlage of the Seven Banquets in the "Letter of Aristeas to Philocrates" ', *Aegyptus* 59 (1979), pp. 127-36.

L. Schiffman, 'The Deuteronomic Paraphrase of the Temple Scroll', *RQ* 15 (1991–92), pp. 543-67.

—'The King, his Guard and the Royal Council in the Temple Scroll', *PAAJR* 54 (1987), pp. 237-59.

—'The Law of Vows and Oaths (Num. 30, 3-16) in the Zadokite Fragments and the Temple Scroll', *RQ* 15 (1991–92), pp. 199-214.

—'The Laws of War in the Temple Scroll', *RQ* 13 (1988), pp. 299-311.

E. Tov, 'Deut. 12 and 11QTemple LII-LIII. A Contrastive Analysis', *RQ* 15 (1991), pp. 169-73.

M. Weinfeld, 'The Royal Guard According to the Temple Scroll', *RB* 87 (1980), pp. 394-96.

4

THE DESCRIPTION OF THE NEW JERUSALEM

Editions, Translations and Bibliographies

Critical Editions of the Aramaic Texts

M. Baillet, 'Description de la Jérusalem Nouvelle', in M. Baillet, J.T. Milik, R. de Vaux (eds.), *Les 'Petites Grottes' de Qumran* (DJD, 3; Oxford: Clarendon Press, 1962), pp. 84-89, pl. xvi.

F. García Martínez, E.J.C. Tigchelaar and A.S. van der Woude, '11QNew Jerusalem ar', in *idem* (eds.), *Qumran Cave 11, II: 11Q2-18, 11Q20-31* (DJD, 23; Oxford: Clarendon Press, 1998), pp. 305-56, pls. xxxv-xl, liii.

J.T. Milik, 'Description de la Jérusalem Nouvelle (?)', in D. Barthélemy and J.T. Milik (eds.), *Qumran Cave 1* (DJD, 1; Oxford: Clarendon Press, 1955), pp. 134-35, pl. xxxi.

—'Description de la Jérusalem Nouvelle', in M. Baillet, J.T. Milik and R. de Vaux (eds.), *Les 'Petites Grottes' de Qumran* (DJD, 3; Oxford: Clarendon Press, 1962), pp. 184-92, pls. xl-xli.

Other Editions

K. Beyer, *Die aramäische Texte von dem Toten Meer* (Göttingen: Vandenhoeck & Ruprecht, 1984), pp. 214-22.

M. Chyutin, *The New Jerusalem Scroll from Qumran: A Comprehensive Reconstruction* (JSPSup, 25; Sheffield: Sheffield Academic Press, 1997).

J. Fitzmyer and D. Harrington, '1Q New Jerusalem', '2Q New Jerusalem', '5Q New Jerusalem', '11Q New Jerusalem', in *idem*, *A Manual of Palestinian Aramaic Texts (Second Century BC–Second Century AD)* (Rome: Biblical Institute Press, 1978), pp. 46-65.

F. García Martínez and E.J.C. Tigchelaar, '1Q32', '2Q24', in *idem, The Dead Sea Scrolls Study Edition* (Leiden: E.J. Brill, 1997), I, pp. 110-13, 218-21.

F. García Martínez and E.J.C. Tigchelaar, '4Q554', '4Q554a', '4Q555', '5Q15', '11Q18', in *idem, The Dead Sea Scrolls Study Edition* (Leiden: E.J. Brill, 1998), II, pp. 1106-11, 1110-13, 1112-13, 1136-41, 1220-27.

E. Tov with the collaboration of S. Pfann (eds.), *The Dead Sea Scrolls on Microfiche: A Comprehensive Facsimile Edition of the Texts from the Judean Desert* (Leiden: E.J. Brill, 1993), 8-11 (1Q32); 86 (2Q24); 78-79 (4Q554); 80 (4Q555); 46 (5Q15); 87-88 (11Q18).

Preliminary Editions, Descriptions and Textual Studies

M. Baillet, 'Fragments araméens de Qumrân 2: description de la Jérusalem Nouvelle', *RB* 62 (1955), pp. 222-45, pls. ii-iii.
F. García Martínez, 'The Last Surviving Columns of 11QNJ', in F. García Martínez *et al.* (eds.), *The Scriptures and the Scrolls: Studies in Honour of A.S. van der Woude on the Occasion of his 65th Birthday* (VTSup, 49; Leiden: E.J. Brill, 1992), pp. 178-92.
—'More Fragments of 11QNJ', in D. Parry, E. Ulrich (eds.), *The Provo International Conference on the Dead Sea Scrolls: New Texts, Reformulated Issues, and Technological Innovations* (Leiden: E.J. Brill, 1998), pp. 186-98.
J. Greenfield, 'The Small Caves of Qumran', *JAOS* 89 (1969), pp. 132-35.
B. Jongeling, 'Publication provisoire d'un fragment provenant de la grotte 11 de Qumrân (11QJérNouv ar)', *JSJ* 1 (1970), pp. 58-64.
E. Puech, 'A propos de la Jérusalem Nouvelle d'après les manuscrits de la mer Morte', *Semitica* 43-44 (1995), pp. 87-102.
J. Starcky, 'Jérusalem et les manuscrits de la mer Morte', *Le monde de la Bible* 1 (1977), pp. 38-40.

Translations

E. Cook, 'A Vision of the New Jerusalem (1Q32, 2Q24, 4Q554-555, 5Q15, 11Q18)', in M. Wise, M. Abegg and E. Cook (eds.), *The Dead Sea Scrolls: A New Translation* (New York: HarperCollins, 1996), pp. 180-84.
R. Eisenman and M. Wise, 'The New Jerusalem (4Q554)', in *idem*, *The Dead Sea Scrolls Uncovered* (Harmondsworth: Penguin Books, 1992), pp. 39-46.
F. García Martínez, 'Descripción de la Nueva Jerusalén: 2QNueva Jerusalén, 4QNueva Jerusalén^a, 4QNueva Jerusalén^b, 5QNueva Jerusalén, 11QNueva Jerusalén', in *idem*, *Textos de Qumrán* (Madrid: Editorial Trotta, 1992), pp. 178-83.
—'Description of the New Jerusalem', in *idem*, *The Dead Sea Scrolls Translated:The Qumran Texts in English* (trans. W. Watson; Leiden: E.J. Brill, 1994), pp. 129-35.
G. Vermes, 'The New Jerusalem (4Q554-5, 5Q15, 1Q32, 2Q24, 4Q232, 11Q18)', in *idem*, *The Complete Dead Sea Scrolls in English* (New York: Penguin Books, 4th edn, 1997), pp. 568-70.

Bibliographies

J.A. Fitzmyer, S.J., *The Dead Sea Scrolls: Major Publications and Tools for Study* (SBL Resources for Biblical Study, 20; rev. edn; Atlanta, GA: Scholars Press, 1990).
F. García Martínez and D.W. Parry, *Bibliography of the Finds in the Desert of Judah 1970–1995* (STDJ, 19; Leiden: E.J. Brill, 1996).
A. Pinnick, Weekly up-dated on-line bibliography of the Dead Sea Scrolls 1995 to the present, *The Orion Center for the Study of the Dead Sea Scrolls and Associated Literature Website*: http://www.orion.mscc.huji.ac.il

1. Description of the Manuscripts

The composition known as 'The Description of the New Jerusalem' (NJ) was found in seven copies in five of the 11 caves in the vicinity of the settlement at Qumran. All seven copies are written in Aramaic; although it was once thought that one or more Hebrew copies might exist (4Q232, 4Q365a), these have been determined to be other compositions (García Martínez 1999: 445 n. 28).

a. 1Q32 ('Description de la Jérusalem Nouvelle (?)')
This manuscript survives in 32 fragments, only seven of which have been identified with any certainty. Its paleographic date lies in the second half of the first century BCE.

b. 2Q24 ('Description de la Jérusalem Nouvelle')
This manuscript survives in 11 fragments, and dates paleographically to the first half of the first century CE. Fragment 1 contains a description of the city. A description of the distribution of the shewbread is found on frag. 4, which overlaps with frag. 20 of the Cave 11 manuscript. Fragments 5-8 preserve material relating to the altar.

c. 4Q554
This manuscript, which has not yet appeared in a critical edition, consists of 14 fragments, with a paleographic date in the second half of the first century BCE. Fragments 1 and 2 each contain the remains of three columns. Fragment 1, which overlaps with 2Q24, frag. 1 and 5Q15, frag. 1, describes the gates and the walls of the city. Columns 1 and 2 of frag. 2 continue the description of the gate entrances and the towers. Fragment 2, col. 3, which begins a new sheet of leather, contains material which seems to describe an eschatological conflict between Israel and the nations, and may not follow immediately after col. 2 (García Martínez 1999: 447-48). An interesting feature of this manuscript is the use of ciphers rather than words to indicate numbers.

d. 4Q554a
Originally grouped with 4Q554, this large fragment has been designated as a separate manuscript by its editor (Puech 1995: 88 n. 1). It also dates to the second half of the first century BCE, and describes the houses in the residential area. It contains an overlap with 5Q15, frag. 1.

e. 4Q555

Only three small fragments remain of this manuscript, which dates to the second half of the first century BCE. Because of the fragmentary nature of the material, its identification as a copy of the New Jerusalem is not completely certain.

f. 5Q15 ('Description de la Jérusalem Nouvelle')

Copied at the end of the first century BCE, this manuscript consists of 39 small fragments, 20 of which have been pieced together into two consecutive columns and labelled frag. 1. This reconstructed fragment contains overlaps with 2Q24, frag. 1; 4Q554, frag. 1; and 4Q554a. It describes the residential area of the city, including the insula or city blocks, the streets, and the houses.

g. 11Q18 ('Description of the New Jerusalem')

This manuscript was discovered as a complete scroll in Cave 11. It was evidently wrapped in a cloth (wool?) when it was stored in the cave. Unfortunately, at the time of its discovery the scroll was almost completely petrified and could not be unrolled; its original editor, J. van der Ploeg described it as so hardened that 'it could be mistaken for stones' (García Martínez, Tigchelaar and van der Woude 1998: 306). Thus, only 37 fragments were recovered from a 'protuberance' at the top of the scroll, and their order is uncertain. The paleographic date of the manuscript falls in the first half of the first century CE. The recovered fragments are mainly concerned with the temple and its cult; they contain one overlap with 2Q24, frag. 4, the distribution of the shewbread. The fragments of 11Q18 have been renumbered several times; in this *Guide* I have used the fragment numbers from the critical edition in Garciá Martínez, Tigchelaar and van der Woude 1998.

2. The Contents of 'The Description of the New Jerusalem'

Taken together, the fragments of the extant copies represent a good proportion of the original composition, perhaps as much as half (Chyutin 1997: 9). Thus we can acquire a good general idea of the contents of the New Jerusalem, although most of the details remain difficult to ascertain. The composition is presented as a guided tour of a city which is assumed to be Jerusalem (although, as in the Temple Scroll, the name 'Jerusalem' is never explicitly mentioned) and its Temple, its furnishings and cult, by a heavenly guide to an unnamed seer:

> And he led me to the interior of the city and me[asured each bl]ock, length and breadth; ... Also he showed me all the measurements of all the blocks ... (4Q554, frag. 1, col. 2.12, 15).

According to the original editors, the tour begins outside the city wall and moves inward toward the Temple, finishing with a description of the Temple's furnishings and certain rituals. This order is the same as that of Ezekiel 40–48, and is based on the shape and order of the fragments of the individual manuscripts (see Milik 1962a: 185). Recently, however, Chyutin has argued that the tour begins with the Temple and its furnishings and moves outward, ending with a description of the city walls, as in the Temple Scroll. He bases his reconstruction on the fact that the fragments of 11Q18, which come from somewhere on the outside of the scroll, are concerned with the Temple and its furnishings. If 11Q18 was rolled so that its beginning was on the outside, as was, e.g., the Temple Scroll, then the material concerning the Temple must have come from the beginning of the scroll (Chyutin 1997: 144). Unfortunately, since 11Q18 was petrified, we do not know the direction in which it was rolled. Thus, the direction of the heavenly tour (from the city wall to the Temple or from the Temple to the city wall) cannot be definitively determined. I will follow the majority of the editors and begin with the city wall.

The heavenly tour guide reveals a city wall that contains 12 gates, named after the sons of Jacob (4Q554, frag. 1, cols. 1–2, ll. 11-22, 7-11): Simeon, Levi, Judah on the east; Joseph, Bejamin, Reuben on the south; Issachar, Zebulon, Gad on the west; and Dan, Naphtali, Asher on the north (Puech 1995: 94, partially reconstructed). This is very similar but not identical to the order of the gates of the middle and outer courts in the Temple Scroll (contra Wise 1990a: 78): Simeon, Levi, Judah on the east; Reuben, Joseph, Bejamin on the south; Issachar, Zebulon, Gad on the west; and Dan, Naphtali, Asher on the north (cols. 39–41). The gates are flanked by towers. The guide gives very precise measurements, as he will throughout the composition, in three different units of measurement: the cubit, the reed or rod, and the *ris*. This is in contrast to the Temple Scroll, which generally uses the cubit and once the *ris* (col. 52.18), but not the reed; and Ezekiel, who generally uses the cubit, once the reed (40.5-7), but not the *ris*. The reed equals seven cubits (it is a matter of some debate whether the cubit in the New Jerusalem was the royal cubit of 52 cm or the common cubit of 45 cm), and the *ris* equals 352 cubits. The city wall measures 140 × 100 *ris* (4Q554, frag. 1, cols. 1–2); thus the city in the New Jerusalem is rectangular, unlike the city in Ezekiel or the temple complex in the Temple Scroll, which are squares.[1] According to Broshi (1995: 12), 140 × 100

---

1. Licht (1979: 49) argued for a square city based on the description in Ezekiel,

4. The Description of the New Jerusalem

ris would equal approximately 6300 sq. km, a gigantic city larger by far than most modern cities, including present-day Jerusalem!

Inside the wall the city is divided by streets running parallel and perpendicular to one another, thus forming city blocks or insula. There are six large avenues: three run east to west, and three from south to north; the widest is the middle south–north avenue, which is 92 cubits wide (4Q554, frag. 1, col. 2, ll. 15-22; 5Q15, frag. 1, ll. 2-7). The streets divide the city into residential blocks; each block contains 60 two-storied houses. There are 4,480 blocks, for a total of 28,800 houses in the city. The heavenly guide gives the measurements for the blocks, their gates and staircases, the houses and their courtyards (2Q24, frag. 1; 4Q554, frag. 1, col. 3; 4Q554a; 5Q15, frag. 1, cols. 1–2), as well as the interior of a house, which includes 22 dining couches on the lower level (4Q554a, l. 8; 5Q15, frag. 1, col. 2, l. 11). If the number 22 reflects the number of inhabitants per house, then the population of the city would be 650,000, larger than most cities of the ancient world, with the exception of very large cities like Rome and Alexandria. It is also possible, however, that the number of couches reflects the number of pilgrims expected in the city during festivals such as Passover or Sukkot, when the population would swell (García Martínez 1999: 453).

The description of the Temple complex (2Q24, 11Q18) is unfortunately extremely fragmentary. The Temple appears to be located to the south of the main east–west street of the city, within the city walls (4Q554, frag. 1, col. 2, l. 18; 5Q15, frag. 1, col. 1, ll. 3-4). There may be two courtyards; 11Q18, frag. 6 contains the measurement '280 cubits' (the measurement of the inner court of the Temple in the Temple Scroll [col. 36]), which may indicate the presence of an inner court wall. 2Q24, frag. 3, mentions a 'sapphire door' and a wall; sapphire is a precious stone, which may indicate that this door leads into the Temple complex. Inside the court sits an altar with four horns (2Q24, frag. 7; 11Q18, frags. 13, 22). The Temple itself probably has two stories (11Q18, frag. 9, l. 1), and contains an altar for the shewbread (2Q24, frag. 4; 11Q18, frag. 8) and a throne of some kind (11Q18, frags. 31, col. 2; 33). There are references to gold and precious gems (11Q18, frags. 8; 10, col. 1; 11); evidently all the buildings in the Temple complex were to be decorated with gold. There is very little else concerning the architecture of the Temple that can be gleaned with any certainty from the fragments. The fragments also refer to some of the paraphernalia of the Temple cult: wheels and pillars (1Q32), sieves, cups, bowls

---

but he did not have access to the Cave 4 fragments, which clearly state the measurements of the city wall. Chyutin (1994: 95) also argued for a square city, but in his 1997 publication (p. 77, fig. 6) he has altered his position.

and cauldrons (11Q18, frags. 12, col. 1; 18). Most interesting are the allusions to the garments of the high priest, especially the crowns, which seem to be a part of some specific ritual:

> And the fif[th] crown[...] the inside of a palm flower. And the sixth crown [...] the seventh is like a blossom [...] the chief priest will be clothed [(11Q18, frag. 14).

The New Jerusalem scroll also contains references to certain festivals and Temple rituals. The Passover is discussed in 11Q18, frags. 16, col. 2 and 27, while the Sabbath and New Moon appear in 11Q18, frag. 19. 11Q18, frag. 15, contains a description of the changing of the divisions of the priests; note that l. 4 contains the number 'twenty-six'. If this number refers to the divisions of the priests or the period of their service, which seems likely (García Martínez, Tigchelaar, van der Woude 1998: 330), it indicates that the New Jerusalem scroll presupposes the solar calendar, as in other Qumran documents (see 1QM, col. 2.1-2; cf. 1 Chron. 24.7-18, where the priests are divided into *twenty-four* lots).[2] The most extensively preserved description of a Temple ceremony is that of the distribution of the shewbread:

> 1. eve]ry seventh day before God, a memori[al offering ...
> 2. bread. And they shall take the bread] outside the Temple, to the right of its west side, [and it shall be divided ...
> 3. And while I was watching, it was distrib]uted to the eighty-four priests [...
> 3a.] from all; the division of the tables was satisfied
> 4. ... th]em and fourteen prie[sts ...
> 5. the priests; two loave]s [upon] which was the incense
> 6. ... and while I was watching, one of the two loaves was g]iven to the ch[ief] priest [...
> 7. with him; and the other was given to the second who was stan]ding close to him [...
> (11Q18, frag. 20, ll. 1-7; also 2Q24, frag. 4, ll. 9-16).

The bread, after it has been displayed in the Temple for a week, is taken outside and distributed to the priests in their divisions, beginning with the high priest. This ceremony is based on Lev. 24.5-9:

> You shall take choice flour, and bake twelve loaves of it; two-tenths of an ephah shall be in each loaf. You shall place them in two rows, six in a row, on the table of pure gold. You shall put pure frankincense with each row, to be a token offering for the bread, as an offering by fire to the LORD. Every sabbath day Aaron shall set them in order before the LORD regularly as a commitment

---

2. The evidence from Qumran concerning the number of priestly courses is mixed; for example, the 'Calendrical Documents' [4Q320-330] discuss the 24 (rather than 26) priestly courses. For a thorough discussion of this problem, see Glessmer 1999: 223-33.

4. The Description of the New Jerusalem   73

of the people of Israel, as a covenant forever. They shall be for Aaron and his descendants, who shall eat them in a holy place, for they are most holy portions for him from the offerings by fire to the LORD, a perpetual due.

Finally, 4Q554, frag. 2, col. 3 discusses an eschatological war between Israel and its enemies:

> 15. after it, and the kingdom of ... [... and the kingdom of]
> 16. the Kittim after it, all of them; at the end of all of them [...]
> 17. others who are great and powerful with them [...]
> 18. with them Edom and Moab and the sons of Ammon [...]
> 19. of Babel, all its land which shall not ... [...]
> 20. and they shall harm your descendants until the time that [...]
> 21. with all ... [...] the kingdom of [...] which n[ot ...]
> 22. and the peoples shall d[o] with them [...]

That this conflict takes place at the end of time seems certain in light of the phrases 'at the end of all of them' and 'your descendants'. The enemies are traditional; Israel had skirmishes with Ammon, Edom and Moab during the period of the wilderness wanderings (Num. 20.14-21; 22.1-3; Deut. 23.3-6), while the Kittim are sea-faring peoples mentioned in later periods (e.g. Dan. 11.30), who become identified with the Romans in Qumran literature (e.g. Pesher Habakkuk, Pesher Nahum). Babylon is, of course, the empire responsible for destroying the kingdom of Judah and razing Jerusalem and its Temple in 587 BCE (2 Kgs 25.1-17). The Kittim, Ammon, Moab and Edom appear in the War Scroll (col. 1.1-7) as among the enemies the Sons of Light will defeat in the final cosmic war. The relationship of this material to the rest of the New Jerusalem scroll is, however, problematic, since it contains no mention of the Temple or the city. It is even questionable whether it belongs to the same composition, or is part of another, otherwise unknown, eschatological work.

3. Genre, Date and Provenance

a. Genre
The genre of the Description of the New Jerusalem is that of an apocalypse. The literary fiction of the work is that it is a vision given to a seer by a presumably heavenly tour guide, although the identities of both the seer and the guide are unfortunately not preserved in the fragments. The seer is shown the vision by the heavenly mediator, indicated by such phrases as 'and he showed me', 'and he led me'. He is also shown a book (11Q18, frag. 19), which, despite its enigmatic nature, is further evidence that the seer is receiving a heavenly revelation. Chyutin (1997: 52-55) argues that this is part of the ritual of the Temple, the 'Reading from the

Book' ceremony, but this is a misunderstanding of the text. The vision of the eschatological Jerusalem is a familiar one in apocalyptic literature (Rev. 21.9-27; *4 Ezra* 10.25-28). Further, if 4Q554, frag. 2, col. 3 does belong to the New Jerusalem scroll, the scroll contains a description of an eschatological battle. All of these factors justify categorizing the Description of the New Jerusalem as an apocalypse (Collins 1999: 417-18; García Martínez 1999: 452-53).

This has an impact on our understanding of the purpose of the Scroll. The temple and city it is describing is a future, ideal temple, for the time of the eschaton. It is not necessarily built with human hands, although there is no indication in the text about who is to build the temple. Thus, the temple and cult of the New Jerusalem are different in kind from the normative temple and cult of the Temple Scroll, which is meant to be built by human hands and exist in historic time. In fact, a reader of both the Temple Scroll and the New Jerusalem (a distinct possibility, since copies of each were found in both Caves 4 and 11) might understand the New Jerusalem text to be describing the temple God will erect on 'the day of creation, when I shall create my temple, establishing it for myself for all days, according to the covenant which I made with Jacob at Bethel' (11QTemple[a], col. 29.9-10). As another possibility, García Martínez (1999: 453-55) argues that the New Jerusalem can be understood as describing the temple referred to in 4QFlorilegium, which shall be built 'in the last days' (4Q174, frags. 1-3, col. 1.2), or the eschatological temple in the War Scroll (1QM, col. 2.1-6). Thus the Description of the New Jerusalem would play an important part in the apocalyptic musings of the Qumran community.

b. Date and Provenance

The question of the date of the Description of the New Jerusalem has yet to be satisfactorily answered. The earliest copies of the text are from the second half of the first century BCE (50–11 BCE); therefore the composition of the work must be earlier than 50 BCE. Various dates have been proposed: 200 BCE (Broshi), 170 BCE (Wise), 200–150 BCE (García Martínez), and 142 BCE (Beyer). All of these dates (with the exception of Beyer's) fall within the first half of the second century BCE; it may be difficult to narrow the date beyond that. The work is written in what Greenfield has termed Standard Literary Aramaic, which functioned as a written dialect throughout the Hasmonaean period, and therefore cannot help us pinpoint a more precise date (Wise 1990a: 87 n. 90). Broshi (1995: 18) and Licht (1979: 48) have argued that underlying the city plan of the New Jerusalem was a Hippodamian street plan, in which the marketplace (*agora*) is the center of the city with the main street from the city gate leading to it, and the remaining streets laid out in a grid around it. In this case the scroll would have been composed after the conquest of the east by Alexander (332 BCE). It is also possible that the plan underlying the New Jerusalem is that of the Roman *castrum*. In this plan, a main road, the *decumans maximus*, ran lengthwise through the camp, and another, the *cardo maximus*, ran perpendicular to it, with the secondary streets arranged in a grid around it (Chyutin 1997: 123). If this is the plan underlying the New Jerusalem, its composition would be placed in the latter half of the first century BCE, after the conquest of Pompey (63 BCE). However, Chyutin (1997: 126-27) has recently argued that the city plan is actually based on the archaic Egyptian method of city building, and thus is not helpful for dating. Other architectural elements, nevertheless, may still place the New Jerusalem in the later Hellenistic period: the tower with the spiral staircase and the peristyle courtyard (Broshi 1995: 18). This leaves us with a probable date of composition sometime between 200–100 BCE.

The question of the scroll's place of origin is no less unsettled. That the work was popular at Qumran is certain from the presence of seven copies in five caves. García Martínez has argued that in fact the New Jerusalem is a Qumranic apocalypse (García Martínez 1992c: 212). However, the text contains none of what has been classified as typical Qumran sectarian ideas (dualism, predeterminism, etc.). Wise, in fact, suggests that the New Jerusalem predates the Qumran community, although it stems from the priestly or scribal circles that gave rise to that community (Wise 1990a: 81-86). Puech (1995: 102) is even more cautious, arguing only for composition in Palestine during the Hellenistic period. The use of Aramaic does point to Palestine as the place of origin, while the apocalyptic genre and the interest in the Temple and its cult indicate an apocalyptic priestly group, possibly the forerunners of those who crystallized into the Qumran community (see also García Martínez 1999: 453-54).

Further Reading

M. Broshi, 'Visionary Architecture and Town Planning in the Dead Sea Scrolls', in D. Dimant and L. Schiffman (eds.), *Time to Prepare the Way in the Wilderness: Papers on the Qumran Scrolls* (Leiden: E.J. Brill, 1995), pp. 9-22.

M. Chyutin, 'The New Jerusalem: Ideal City', *DSD* 1 (1994), pp. 71-97.

—*The New Jerusalem Scroll from Qumran: A Comprehensive Reconstruction* (JSPSup, 25; Sheffield: Sheffield Academic Press, 1997).

F. García Martínez, 'The 'New Jerusalem' and the Future Temple of the Manuscripts from Qumran', in *idem, Qumran and Apocalyptic: Studies on the Aramaic Texts from Qumran* (Leiden: E.J. Brill, 1992), pp. 180-213.

—'The Temple Scroll and the New Jerusalem', in P. Flint and J. VanderKam (eds.), *The Dead Sea Scrolls after Fifty Years: A Comprehensive Assessment* (2 vols.; Leiden: E.J. Brill, 1999), II, pp. 431-60.

J. Licht, 'An Ideal Town Plan from Qumran: The Description of the New Jerusalem', *IEJ* 29 (1979), pp. 45-59.
E. Puech, 'A propos de la Jérusalem Nouvelle d'après les manuscrits de la mer Morte', *Semitica* 43-44 (1995), pp. 89-102.
M. Wise, 'The Temple Source and the New Jerusalem Text', in *idem, A Critical Study of the Temple Scroll from Qumran Cave 11* (SAOC, 49; Chicago: Oriental Institute of the University of Chicago, 1990), pp. 64-86.

5

THE TEMPLE SCROLL AND OTHER SECOND TEMPLE JEWISH LITERATURE

This chapter will provide comparisons between the Temple Scroll and other Second Temple Jewish literature, focusing particularly on other documents found in the caves at Qumran. I will stress the similarities rather than the differences; many of these similarities have been discussed in previous chapters; they are collected here for convenient reference. It is important to note that none of the preserved texts from Qumran contains a recognizable quotation of the Temple Scroll. The readers of this *Guide* should remember that the Temple Scroll is most dependent on and similar to the Torah (Pentateuch), on which it is based; similarities to any other documents pale by comparison.

1. Jubilees

The book of *Jubilees* belongs to the genre 'Rewritten Bible', since it is a retelling, in a polemical style and with embellishments, of Genesis 1–Exodus 15. Its fictional setting is on Mt Sinai, where an angel of the presence gives the book to Moses (*Jub.* 1.27-28). The similarity to the Temple Scroll is obvious, although the Temple Scroll presents God speaking directly to Moses, without an angelic intermediary. Although no scholarly consensus exists on the date of *Jubilees*, a date somewhere between 168/7–152 BCE seems preferable (Charlesworth 1985: 197). It was composed in Hebrew, probably in Palestine. *Jubilees* was discovered in 14 manuscripts (plus three related texts) in five caves at Qumran, a number which attests to its importance to the Qumran community. In addition, it is cited by name in the Damascus Document (CD 16.2b-4a).

There are many similarities between the book of *Jubilees* and the Temple Scroll. Some of them are broad and extend throughout both texts: both embrace the 364-day solar calendar, and both give particular prominence to Levi and/or the Levites (*Jub.* 31.15; 32.3-9; 45.15; for the Temple Scroll see Chapter 3).

Some of the similarities are more specific: the celebration of the Spring New Year on the first of Nisan (*Jub.* 7.2-3; 27.19; 11QTemple^a, col. 14.9); the regulations for the Passover, which in both documents is to be offered by any male over the age of 20 and must be eaten in the Temple courts (*Jub.* 29.1, 10-20; 11QTemple^a, col. 17.6-9); the celebration of the Feast of Weeks as a first-fruits festival (*Jub.* 6.21; 11QTemple^a, col. 19.9), during which the second tithe is brought (*Jub.* 32.10-15; 11QTemple^a, col. 43.4-10); and the presentation of a special wood offering (*Jub.* 21.13-14; 11QTemple^a, cols. 23-25.2) (Brooke 1988b: 37). Altogether the similarities are so extensive that it is probable that the two documents stem from the same exegetical, cultic tradition (VanderKam 1989: 232). However, the differences between the two documents, including the pseudepigraphical fiction and the narrative style as well as differences in detail, make Wacholder's thesis that the two works were orginally two halves of a single 'Book of the Law' highly unlikely (Wacholder 1985: 205).

2. *Miqṣat Ma'aśē ha-Torah*

Miqṣat Ma'aśē ha-Torah (4QMMT) is an important text for understanding halakhic controversies in the Second Temple period. It was discovered in six copies from Cave 4, Qumran; the oldest copy dates to c. 75 BCE. There is general agreement that its date of composition lies in the first half of the second century BCE (Qimron and Strugnell 1994: 113, 121). The structure somewhat resembles that of a letter: a 'we' group (the author[s]) addresses a 'you' (a leader of Israel, presumably a high priest) to argue against the halakhic positions of a 'they' group (probably the Pharisees; Qimron and Strugnell 1994: 114-15). There is a tripartite division of the contents: Section A lays out a festival calendar based on the 364-day solar calendar; Section B is a list of halakhic controversies; and Section C is a hortatory closing. The purpose of 4QMMT is to convince the recipient of the correctness of the author(s)'s halakhic positions. It contains several similarities to the Temple Scroll, making it extremely likely that the two compositions were written in the same milieu.

The first area of agreement is the festival calendar. 4QMMT A preserves the reckoning for the Feast of Weeks and the first-fruits festivals of wheat, wine and oil which corresponds to the reckoning in the Temple Scroll, including the understanding of the word 'Sabbath' as the seventh day (Saturday; see p. 52 above) (Glessmer 1999: 239-40):

> i. [The sixteenth (day) of it (i.e. the second month) is a Sabbath]. The twenty third of it is a Sabbath. The thirtieth [of it is a Sabbath. The seventh of the third (month) is a Sabbath. The fourteenth of it is a Sabbath. The fifteenth of it is the Festival of Weeks. The twenty-
>
> ii. fi]rst of it is a Sabbath. The twenty-eighth of it is a Sabbath. After it (i.e. the Sabbath), Sunday and Monday, [Tuesday is to be added (to this month). And the season terminates-ninety-one days. The first of the fourth (month) is a Memorial Day. The fourth]
>
> iii. of it [is a Sabbath]. The el[eventh] of it is a Sabbath. The eighteenth of it is a Sabbath. The twenty-fifth of it is a Sabbath. The second of the fif[th (month) is a Sabbath. The third of it is the Festival of the (New) Wine...
>
> iv. The ninth of it is a Sabbath]. The sixteenth of it is a Sabbath. The twenty-third of it is a Sabbath. The thirtieth [of it is a Sabbath. The seventh of the sixth (month) is a Sabbath. The fourteenth of it is a Sabbath. The twenty-first]
>
> v. of it is a Sabbath. The twenty-second of it is the Festival of the (New) Oil, on the day af[ter the Sab]bath. Af[ter it] is [the Wood] Offer[ing... (Qimron and Strugnell 1994: 45).

This calendar also relates 4QMMT to the book of *Jubilees*.

The second area of agreement is found in the halakhic controversies reflected in 4QMMT. Although the tone of the Temple Scroll is generally not polemical but matter-of-fact, that of 4QMMT is polemical, albeit mildly, and its polemic is directed at those who hold positions later identified with the Pharisees. The following list indicates those areas in which 4QMMT and the Temple Scroll overlap:

1. The consumption of the offering. 4QMMT B 9–13 and 11QTemple[a], col. 20.11-13 mandate the consumption of the edible parts of a shelamim sacrifice on the day it is offered, before the sun goes down. The rabbis allowed consumption until midnight (*m. Men.* 1.3-4).
2. Ritual impurity. According to both 4QMMT (B 13–17, 64–72) and the Temple Scroll (45.9-10; 49.19-21; 51.2-5), anyone in a state of ritual impurity remains completely impure until the sun sets, even after immersion. However, according to the Pharisees, an impure person became pure for all but the most proscribed ritual activities after immersion but before sunset. This became known in rabbinic times as the concept of *tevûl yôm* (Schiffman 1989–90: 438). The position of 4QMMT and the Temple Scroll corresponds to the plain sense of the biblical text (Lev. 11.29-38; Num. 19.9); therefore it is

difficult to be certain whether or not they are explicitly polemicizing against the concept of *ṭevûl yôm*, although they certainly would have rejected it (Grabbe 1997: 91-92).

3. The purity of hides. 4QMMT B 18–20 seems to prohibit the hides of clean animals in the Temple if they were slaughtered outside the Temple. This corresponds to 11QTemple[a], col. 47.7-18, which forbids bringing the skins of any animal not slaughtered in the Temple into the Temple complex.
4. The slaughter of pregnant animals. Both 4QMMT B 36–38 and 11QTemple[a], col. 52.5-7 prohibit the slaughter of pregnant animals, based on Lev. 22.28.
5. Regulations concerning the blind. The Temple Scroll forbids the blind to enter the Temple (45.12-13) because of the risk of defilement; 4QMMT B 49-54 requests that the blind and the deaf 'revere the Temple' (i.e. do not enter it) since they do not know how to obey the law.
6. Priestly gifts. According to 4QMMT B 62-64 and 11QTemple[a], col. 60.2-4, the fruits of the fourth year and the tithe of cattle and sheep and goats belong to the priests. This agrees with *Jubilees*, Tobit, Philo and the Karaites. However, the rabbis decreed that these should be offered in Jerusalem and consumed by the owner (fourth-year produce: *m. Ma'as. Š.* 5.3; tithe of cattle: *m. Zeb.* 5.8; Schiffman 1989–90: 452-56).
7. Contact with a bone. 4QMMT B 72-74 states that any bone, whether or not it contains flesh, renders corpse impurity. This agrees with 11QTemple[a], col. 50.4-6, which decrees that anyone who touches the bone of a dead person has contracted corpse impurity.

3. Damascus Document

The Damascus Document (CD, 4QD) was first discovered in two medieval copies at the end of the nineteenth century in the Cairo *genizah*. Subsequently fragments of ten copies of the Damascus Document were discovered in Caves 4, 5 and 6 at Qumran. The oldest copies date to the second half of the first century BCE. The Damascus Document probably reached its final form towards the end of the second century BCE, although it certainly contains older source material and went through several stages of redaction (Hempel 2000). It contains many important parallels with the Temple Scroll, indicating that both compositions originated in the same levitical priestly circles. Some of these parallels are general in nature:

the Damascus Document espouses the 364-day solar calendar, as indicated by its citation of *Jubilees* in CD 16.2b-4a. It also promotes the interests of the Levites as a separate class, distinguishing them from the priests and the people (CD 3.21–4.12; 10.14–11.18; 13.3-7). Most of the parallels, however, occur in the legal sections of the Damascus Document.

1. Sexual purity. The Temple Scroll (45.11-12) forbids entrance into the Temple city by any man who has had sexual intercourse resulting in ejaculation. The Damascus Document prohibits intercourse in the Temple city (CD 12.1-2). The wording is slightly different, but the result is the same: sexual intercourse is forbidden in the Temple city.
2. Slaughter of pregnant animals. 4QD^e 2.2.15 forbids the slaughter of pregnant animals, as does 11QTemple^a, col. 52.5-7 (and 4QMMT B 36-38).
3. Prohibition of polygamy and divorce. CD 4.20–5.5 prohibits polygamy ('taking two wives') and, evidently, divorce ('in their lives'). The Temple Scroll, as we have seen in Chapter 3, certainly prohibits polygamy and divorce for the king (57.15-19). It is interesting that the Damascus Document singles out King David as someone who unintentionally transgressed this commandment.
4. Priestly gifts. 11QTemple^a, col. 60.2-4 gives the fourth-year fruits and the tithe of the cattle, sheep and goats to the priests (also 4QMMT B 62–64). This same ruling is found in 4QD^e 2.2.6-8 and 4QD^a 6.4.
5. Betrothal of a slave woman. 4QD^e 4, 4QD^a 12 (composite text) contains an intriguing parallel to the law of the beautiful captive woman in 11QTemple^a, col. 63.10-15. The Damascus Document rule concerns the betrothal of a female slave, and seems to mandate a waiting period of seven years, which is somehow related to the man's food (ll. 15, 19). According to the Temple Scroll, a captive woman married to an Israelite is barred from the 'pure food' for seven years.
6. Treason. 4QD^e 2.2.13 condemns a man who 'reveals a secret of his people to the Gentiles'. According to 11QTemple^a, col. 64.6-9, capital punishment by crucifixion or hanging is the penalty for treason.
7. Uncle–niece marriage. As noted above in Chapter 3, both the Damascus Document (CD 5.7-11) and the Temple Scroll (66.15-17) prohibit the practice of uncle–niece marriage in no uncertain terms, based on the same exegesis of Lev. 18.12-14.

The similarities among the Temple Scroll, *Jubilees*, 4QMMT and the Damascus Document are extensive enough to posit that all of these texts originated in the same disaffected priestly milieu, the milieu that gave rise to the Qumran sectarian community.[1]

4. The Description of the New Jerusalem

Although the Temple Scroll and the Description of the New Jerusalem treat the same or very similar subjects, namely the ideal Temple and city, the two documents actually have much less in common than the four compared above. Although Wise (1990a: 81-84) has argued that the New Jerusalem text is a source for the Temple Source of the Temple Scroll, this is very unlikely, as shown by García Martínez 1992c: 182-85. Rather, it is possible that both texts drew on common source material, mainly in the area of architectural features (Broshi 1995: 10).

The main instance of similarity is the names of the gates of the middle and outer courts in the Temple Scroll and the city gates in the New Jerusalem, which are practically identical (see above, Chapter 4). Both texts describe a similar stairhouse; the Temple Scroll locates such a stairhouse next to the Temple (cols. 30–31), while the New Jerusalem describes a spiral staircase in the gate of a city block (4Q554, frag. 1, col. 3.20-22; 5Q15, col. 2.2-5). In the description of the Temple in the Temple Scroll, wheels and pillars are mentioned in connection with the slaughterhouse (col. 35); NJ 1Q32 also alludes to wheels and pillars. Both texts contain the measurement '280 cubits', referring to a Temple court (11QTemple[a], col. 36; 11Q18, frag. 6). Outside of the realm of architectural features, the New Jerusalem text appears to mention the Levites performing sacrifices (11Q18, frag. 30), as does the Temple Scroll, col. 22. This role of the Levites in the sacrificial cult elevated their status vis-à-vis the priests, and conforms to a general pattern we have noted in these Second Temple texts found at Qumran of according a higher status to the Levites. Finally, neither text ever mentions the name 'Jerusalem', in keeping with the style of the book of Deuteronomy (VanderKam 1994: 134). These similarities are enough to suppose that the Temple Scroll and the Description of the New Jerusalem had common traditions.

5. Other Compositions

Several other compositions discovered in the caves at Qumran also demonstrate parallels with the Temple Scroll. Possibly the most important is

1. Although there are differences in halakhot among the four texts; for example,

5. *The Temple Scroll and Other Second Temple Jewish Literature* 83

the parallel with 4QReworked Pentateuch^c (4Q365). As discussed in Chapter 3, 4QRP^c frag. 23 mentions the Feast of Oil, then goes on to give a list of the order in which the tribes should bring their offerings for the Wood Festival. This order is an exact parallel to that of the Temple Scroll (cols. 23–24). However, the text of cols. 23–24 is much longer than that of 4QRP^c; 4QRP^c reflects a shorter text (Crawford 1994: 264-65). There are three possibilities to explain the overlap: (1) the Temple Scroll and 4QRP are drawing on common source material; (2) the Temple Scroll is a source for 4QRP; (3) 4QRP is a source for the Temple Scroll (preferred by Stegemann 1988: 252 and Wise 1990a: 50).

Yadin made extensive comparisons of the Temple Scroll and the War Scroll (1QM) in his commentary, but these comparisons have not proved as salient as those with *Jubilees*, 4QMMT and the Damascus Document. The most important comparisons are as follows: the documents share the concept of zones of holiness, the War Scroll in the battle camp, the Temple Scroll surrounding the Temple (both derived from the description of the camp of the wilderness wandering). As a result, both exclude women and boys from the holier areas (1QM 7.3; 11QTemple^a, col. 39.6), and locate the latrines a specific distance away from the pure precincts (1QM 7.6-7; 11QTemple^a, col. 46.13). Further, both the War Scroll and the Temple Scroll provide for an organization composed of 12 priests, 12 Levites and 12 Israelites, the Temple Scroll as the king's council (57.11-13) and in the War Scroll to serve and guard the sanctuary during the eschatological war (1QM 2.1-6; Thiering 1989: 102). It is unlikely that the War Scroll is directly dependent on the Temple Scroll.

Various other texts discovered at Qumran also display parallels with the Temple Scroll. The Astronomical Enoch (found in the Ethiopic *1 Enoch* in chs. 72-82, and at Qumran in manuscripts 4Q209, 210 and 211), which dates no later than the third century BCE, lays out a luni-solar calendar which is probably the basis for the 364-day solar calendar of *Jubilees*, 4QMMT and the Temple Scroll. 4Q327 mentions the Feast of Oil. 4Q251 gives the fourth-year produce to the priests, and prohibits uncle-niece marriage. Other scholars have noted other possible parallels (see bibliography). All of these parallels demonstrate that the Temple Scroll was not an isolated text within the Qumran library, but was part of a constellation of pre-Qumranic literature preserved, copied and studied by the sect at Qumran.

---

see Schiffman (1991–92b) on the laws of vows and oaths in the Temple Scroll and the Damascus Document.

Further Reading: Critical Editions and Translations

Jubilees

M. Baillet, 'Livre des Jubilés (i, ii)', in M. Baillet, J.T. Milik and R. de Vaux (eds.), *Les 'Petites Grottes' de Qumran* (DJD, 3; Oxford: Clarendon Press, 1962), pp. 77-78, pl. xv.

R.H. Charles, *The Book of Jubilees, or the Little Genesis* (Jerusalem: Makor Press, 1972).

F. García Martínez, 'Book of Jubilees', in *idem*, *The Dead Sea Scrolls Translated* (trans. W. Watson; Leiden: E.J. Brill, 1994), pp. 238-45.

F. García Martínez, E.J.C. Tigchelaar and A.S. van der Woude, '11QJubilees', in *idem, Qumran Cave 11, II: 11Q2-18, 11Q20-31* (DJD, 23; Oxford: Clarendon Press, 1998), pp. 207-20, pl. xxvi.

J.T. Milik, '1QJubilees^a' and '1QJubilees^b', in D. Barthélemy and J.T. Milik (eds.), *Qumran Cave 1* (DJD, 1; Oxford: Clarendon Press, 1955), pp. 82-84, pl. xvi.

J. VanderKam and J.T. Milik, 'Jubilees', in H. Attridge *et al.* (eds.), *Qumran Cave 4, VIII: Parabiblical Texts, Part 1* (DJD, 13; Oxford: Clarendon Press, 1994), pp. 1-186, pls. i-xii.

O.S. Wintermute, 'Jubilees (Second Century BC): A New Translation and Introduction', in J.H. Charlesworth (ed.), *The Old Testament Pseudepigrapha. II. Expansions of the 'Old Testament' and Legends, Wisdom and Philosophical Literature, Prayers, Psalms and Odes, Fragments of Lost Judeo-Hellenistic Works* (Garden City, NY: Doubleday, 1985), pp. 35-142.

4QMMT

M. Abegg, 'A Sectarian Manifesto (4QMMT: 4Q394-399)', in M. Wise, M. Abegg and E. Cook (eds.), *The Dead Sea Scrolls: A New Translation* (London: HarperCollins, 1996), pp. 358-64.

F. García Martínez, 'Halakhic Letter', in *idem*, *The Dead Sea Scrolls Translated* (trans. W. Watson; Leiden: E.J. Brill, 1994), pp. 77-85.

F. García Martínez and E.J.C. Tigchelaar, '4Q394-4Q399', in *idem*, *The Dead Sea Scrolls Study Edition* (2 vols.; Leiden: E.J. Brill, 1998), II, pp. 790-805.

E. Qimron and J. Strugnell, *Miqṣat Ma'aśē ha-Torah: Qumran Cave 4, V* (DJD, 10; Oxford: Clarendon Press, 1994).

G. Vermes, 'MMT (Some Observances of the Law) (4Q394-99)', in *idem*, *The Complete Dead Sea Scrolls in English* (New York: Penguin Books, 4th edn, 1997), pp. 220-28.

Damascus Document

M. Baillet, 'Document de Damas', in M. Baillet, J.T. Milik and R. de Vaux (eds.), *Les 'Petites Grottes' de Qumran* (DJD, 3; Oxford: Clarendon Press, 1962), pp. 128-31, pl. xxvi.

J.M. Baumgarten, *The Damascus Document (4Q266-273): Qumran Cave 4, XIII* (DJD, 18; Oxford: Clarendon Press, 1996).

M. Broshi, *The Damascus Document Reconsidered* (Jerusalem: Israel Exploration Society, 1992).

E. Cook, 'The Damascus Document', in M. Wise, M. Abegg and E. Cook (eds.), *The Dead Sea Scrolls: A New Translation* (London: HarperCollins, 1996), pp. 49-74.

F. García Martínez, 'The Damascus Document', in *idem*, *The Dead Sea Scrolls Translated: The Qumran Texts in English* (trans. W. Watson; Leiden: E.J. Brill, 1994), pp. 33-71.

J.T. Milik, 'Document de Damas', in M. Baillet, J.T. Milik and R. de Vaux (eds.), *Les 'Petites Grottes' de Qumran* (DJD, 3; Oxford: Clarendon Press, 1962), p. 181, pl. xxxviii.

S. Schechter, *Documents of Jewish Sectaries*. I. *Fragments of a Zadokite Work* (Cambridge: Cambridge University Press, 1910).
G. Vermes, 'The Damascus Document', in *idem*, *The Complete Dead Sea Scrolls in English* (New York: Penguin Books, 4th edn, 1997), pp. 125-53.

Description of the New Jerusalem
M. Baillet, 'Description de la Jérusalem Nouvelle', in M. Baillet, J.T. Milik and R. de Vaux (eds.), *Les 'Petites Grottes' de Qumran* (DJD, 3; Oxford: Clarendon Press, 1962), pp. 84-89, pl. xvi.
E. Cook, 'A Vision of the New Jerusalem (1Q32, 2Q24, 4Q554-555, 5Q15, 11Q18)', in M. Wise, M. Abegg and E. Cook (eds.), *The Dead Sea Scrolls: A New Translation* (New York: HarperCollins, 1996), pp. 180-84.
F. García Martínez, 'Description of the New Jerusalem', in *idem*, *The Dead Sea Scrolls Translated: The Qumran Texts in English* (trans. W. Watson; Leiden: E.J. Brill, 1994), pp. 129-35.
F. García Martínez, E.J.C. Tigchelaar and A.S. van der Woude, '11QNew Jerusalem ar', in *idem*, *Qumran Cave 11, II: 10Q2-18, 11Q20-31* (DJD, 23; Oxford: Clarendon Press, 1998), pp. 305-56, pls. xxxv-xl, liii.
J.T. Milik, 'Description de la Jérusalem Nouvelle (?)', in D. Barthélemy and J.T. Milik (eds.), *Qumran Cave 1* (DJD, 1; Oxford: Clarendon Press, 1955), pp. 134-35, pl. xxxi.
—'Description de la Jérusalem Nouvelle', in M. Baillet, J.T. Milik and R. de Vaux (eds.), *Les 'Petites Grottes' de Qumran* (DJD, 3; Oxford: Clarendon Press, 1962), pp. 184-92, pls. xl-xli.
G. Vermes, 'The New Jerusalem (4Q554-5, 5Q15, 1Q32, 2Q24, 4Q232, 11Q18)', in *idem*, *The Complete Dead Sea Scrolls in English* (New York: Penguin Books, 4th edn, 1997), pp. 568-70.

Other Compositions
M. Baillet, 'La guerre des fils de lumière contre les fils de ténèbres', in *idem*, *Qumrân Grotte 4, III (4Q482-4Q520)* (DJD, 7; Oxford: Clarendon Press, 1982), pp. 12-68, pls. v-viii, x, xii, xiv, xvi, xviii, xxiv.
J. Duhaime, 'War Scroll', in J.H. Charlesworth (ed.), *The Dead Sea Scrolls: Hebrew, Aramaic and Greek Texts with English Translations. II. Damascus Document, War Scroll, and Related Documents* (Tübingen: J.C.B. Mohr, 1995), pp. 80-141.
F. García Martínez, 'War Scroll', in *idem*, *The Dead Sea Scrolls Translated: The Qumran Texts in English* (trans. W. Watson; Leiden: E.J. Brill, 1994), pp. 95-122.
J.T. Milik and M. Black, *The Book of Enoch: Aramaic Fragments of Qumran Cave 4* (Oxford: Clarendon Press, 1976).
E.L. Sukenik, '1QWar Scroll', in *idem*, *The Dead Sea Scrolls of the Hebrew University* (Jerusalem: Magnes Press/Hebrew University, 1955), pp. 1-19, pls. 16-34, 47.
E. Tov and S. White, '4QReworked Pentateuch^c', in H. Attridge *et al.* (eds.), *Qumran Cave 4, VIII: Parabiblical Texts, Part 1* (DJD, 13; Oxford: Clarendon Press, 1994), pp. 255-318, pls. xxii-xxxii.

Secondary Literature

General Studies
R.T. Beckwith, 'The Temple Scroll and its Calendar', *RQ* 18 (1997), pp. 3-19.
G. Brin, 'Biblical Laws in the Dead Sea Scrolls', in *idem*, *Studies in Biblical Law: From the Hebrew Bible to the Dead Sea Scrolls* (Sheffield: JSOT Press, 1994), pp. 104-64.

G. Brooke, 'The Temple Scroll—A Law unto Itself?', in B. Lindars (ed.), *Law and Religion: Essays on the Place of the Law in Israel and Early Christianity* (Cambridge: James Clarke, 1988), pp. 34-43, 164-66.

U. Glessmer, 'Calendars in the Qumran Scrolls', in P. Flint and J. VanderKam (eds.), *The Dead Sea Scrolls after Fifty Years: A Comprehensive Assessment* (2 vols.; Leiden: E.J. Brill, 1999), II, pp. 213-78.

S. Talmon, 'The Calendar of the Covenanters of the Judean Desert', in *idem, The World of Qumran from Within: Collected Studies* (Leiden: E.J. Brill, 1990), pp. 147-85.

Jubilees

G. Brin, 'Regarding the Connection between the Temple Scroll and the Book of Jubilees', *JBL* 112 (1992), pp. 108-109.

J.H. Charlesworth, 'The Date of Jubilees and of the Temple Scroll', in Kent Harold Richards (ed.), *SBL Seminar Papers*, 24 (Chico, CA: Scholars Press, 1985), pp. 192-204.

M. Himmelfarb, 'Sexual Relations and Purity in the Temple Scroll and the Book of Jubilees', *DSD* 6 (1999), pp. 11-36.

J. Milgrom, 'The Concept of Impurity in Jubilees and the Temple Scroll', *RQ* 16 (1993), pp. 277-84.

L. Schiffman, 'The Sacrificial System of the Temple Scroll and the Book of Jubilees', *SBL Seminar Papers* 24 (Chico, CA: Scholars Press, 1985), pp. 217-33.

J. VanderKam, 'The Temple Scroll and the Book of Jubilees', in G. Brooke (ed.), *Temple Scroll Studies: Papers Presented at the International Symposium on the Temple Scroll, Manchester, December, 1987* (Sheffield: JSOT Press, 1989), pp. 211-36.

4QMMT

J. Baumgarten, 'Sadducean Elements in Qumran Law', in E. Ulrich and J. VanderKam (eds.), *The Community of the Renewed Covenant: The Notre Dame Symposium on the Dead Sea Scrolls* (Notre Dame: University of Notre Dame Press, 1994), pp. 27-36.

L. Grabbe, '4QMMT and Second Temple Jewish Society', in M. Bernstein, F. García Martínez, J. Kampen (eds.), *Legal Texts and Legal Issues: Proceedings of the Second Meeting of the International Organization for Qumran Studies, Cambridge 1995. Published in Honour of J.M. Baumgarten* (STDJ, 23; Leiden: E.J. Brill, 1997), pp. 89-108.

L. Schiffman, 'Miqsat Ma'aseh ha-Torah and the Temple Scroll', *RQ* 14 (1989–90), pp. 435-57.

—'The New Halakhic Letter (4QMMT) and the Origin of the Dead Sea Sect', in Z. Kapera (ed.), *Mogilany 1989: Papers on the Dead Sea Scrolls Offered in Memory of Jean Carmignac: Part 1, General Research on the Dead Sea Scrolls, Qumran and the New Testament: The Present State of Qumranology* (Cracow: Enigma, 1993), pp. 59-70.

—'Pharisaic and Sadducean Halakhah in Light of the Dead Sea Scrolls: The Case of Tevul Yom', *DSD* 1 (1994), pp. 285-99.

—'The Temple Scroll and the Systems of Jewish Law of the Second Temple Period', in G. Brooke (ed.), *Temple Scroll Studies: Papers Presented at the International Symposium on the Temple Scroll, Manchester, December, 1987* (Sheffield: JSOT Press, 1989), pp. 239-55.

Damascus Document

G. Brin, 'Divorce at Qumran', in M. Bernstein, F. García Martínez and J. Kampen (eds.), *Legal Texts and Legal Issues: Proceedings of the Second Meeting of the International Organization for Qumran Studies, Cambridge 1995. Published in Honour of J.M. Baumgarten* (STDJ, 23; Leiden: E.J. Brill, 1997), pp. 213-44.

5. The Temple Scroll and Other Second Temple Jewish Literature

P. Davies, 'The Temple Scroll and the Damascus Document', in G. Brooke (ed.), *Temple Scroll Studies: Papers Presented at the International Symposium on the Temple Scroll, Manchester, December, 1987* (Sheffield: JSOT Press, 1989), pp. 201-10.

C. Hempel, *The Damascus Texts* (Sheffield: Sheffield Academic Press, 2000).

—*The Laws of the Damascus Document: Sources, Traditions and Redaction* (Leiden: E.J. Brill, 1998).

L.H. Schiffman, 'The Law of Vows and Oaths (Num. 30, 3-16) in the Zadokite Documents and the Temple Scroll', *RQ* 15 (1991–92), pp. 199-214.

Description of the New Jerusalem

M. Broshi, 'Visionary Architecture and Town Planning in the Dead Sea Scrolls', in D. Dimant and L. Schiffman (eds.), *Time to Prepare the Way in the Wilderness: Papers on the Qumran Scrolls* (Leiden: E.J. Brill, 1995), pp. 9-22.

F. García Martínez, 'The Temple Scroll and the New Jerusalem', in P. Flint and J. VanderKam (eds.), *The Dead Sea Scrolls after Fifty Years: A Comprehensive Assessment* (2 vols.; Leiden: E.J. Brill, 1999), II, pp. 431-60.

M. Wise, 'The Temple Source and the New Jerusalem Text', in *idem, A Critical Study of the Temple Scroll from Qumran Cave 11* (SAOC, 49; Chicago: Oriental Institute of the University of Chicago, 1990), pp. 64-86.

Other Compositions

S. Crawford, 'Three Fragments from Qumran Cave 4 and their Relationship to the Temple Scroll', *JQR* 85 (1994), pp. 259-73.

B. Thiering, 'The Date of the Composition of the Temple Scroll', in G. Brooke (ed.), *Temple Scroll Studies: Papers Presented at the International Symposium on the Temple Scroll, Manchester, December, 1987* (Sheffield: JSOT Press, 1989), pp. 99-120.

Cumulative Bibliography

Anderson, Gary
    1992   'The Interpretation of the Purification Offering (חטאת) in the Temple Scroll (11QTemple) and Rabbinic Literature', *JBL* 111: 17-35.

Attridge, Harold, Torleif Elgvin *et al.* (eds.)
    1994   *Qumran Cave 4, VIII: Parabiblical Texts, Part 1* (DJD, 13; Oxford: Clarendon Press).

Baillet, Maurice
    1955   'Fragments araméens de Qumrân 2: Description de la Jérusalem Nouvelle', *RB* 62: 222-45, pls. ii-iii.
    1962a   'Description de la Jérusalem Nouvelle', in Baillet, Milik and de Vaux 1962: 84-89, pl. xvi.
    1962b   'Document de Damas', in Baillet, Milik and de Vaux 1962: 128-31, pl. xxvi.
    1962c   'Livre des Jubilés (i, ii)', in Baillet, Milik and de Vaux 1962: 77-78, pl. xv.
    1982   *Qumrân Grotte 4, III (4Q482-4Q520)* (DJD, 7; Oxford: Clarendon Press).

Baillet, Maurice, J.T. Milik and R. de Vaux (eds.)
    1962   *Les 'Petites Grottes' de Qumran* (DJD, 3; Oxford: Clarendon Press).

Barthélemy, Dominique, and J.T. Milik (eds.)
    1955   *Qumran Cave 1* (DJD, 1; Oxford: Clarendon Press).

Baumgarten, Joseph
    1972   'Does TLH in the Temple Scroll Refer to Crucifixion?', *JBL* 91: 472-81.
    1985   'The First and Second Tithes in the Temple Scroll', in A. Kort and S. Morschauer (eds.), *Biblical and Related Studies Presented to Samuel Iwry* (Winona Lake, IN: Eisenbrauns): 5-15.
    1994   'Sadducean Elements in Qumran Law', in Ulrich and VanderKam 1994: 27-36.
    1996   *The Damascus Document (4Q266-273): Qumran Cave 4, XIII* (DJD, 18; Oxford: Clarendon Press).

Bean, Philip
    1987   'A Theoretical Construct for the Temple of the Temple Scroll' (Master's Thesis; Eugene, OR: University of Oregon).

Beckwith, Roger
    1997   'The Temple Scroll and its Calendar: Their Character and Purpose', *RQ* 18: 3-19.

Bernstein, Moshe J.
    1979   'Midrash Halakhah at Qumran? 11QTemple 64:6-13 and Deuteronomy 21:22-23', *Gesher* 7: 145-66.

Bernstein, Moshe, F. García Martínez and J. Kampen (eds.)
    1997   *Legal Texts and Legal Issues: Proceedings of the Second Meeting of the International Organization for Qumran Studies, Cambridge, 1995. Published in Honour of J.M. Baumgarten* (STDJ, 23: Leiden: E.J. Brill).

Beyer, K.
 1984 *Die aramäische Texte von dem Toten Meer* (Göttingen: Vandenhoeck & Ruprecht).
Boccaccini, Gabriele
 1998 *Beyond the Essene Hypothesis: The Parting of the Ways between Qumran and Enochic Judaism* (Grand Rapids: Eerdmans).
Bogaard, L. van der
 1982 'Le Rouleau du Temple: Quelques remarques concernant les "petits fragments"', in W. Delsman, J. Nelis, J. Peters, W. Römer and A.S. van der Woude (eds.), *Von Kanaan bis Kerala* (AOAT, 211; Kevelaer: Verlag Butzon & Bercker; Neukirchen–Vluyn: Neukirchener Verlag): 285-94.
Bokser, Baruch
 1985 'Approaching Sacred Space', *HTR* 78: 279-99.
Brin, Gershon
 1992 'Regarding the Connection between the Temple Scroll and the Book of Jubilees', *JBL* 112: 108-09.
 1994 *Studies in Biblical Law: From the Hebrew Bible to the Dead Sea Scrolls* (trans. J. Chapman; Sheffield: JSOT Press).
 1997 'Divorce at Qumran', in Bernstein, García Martínez and Kampen 1997: 231-44.
Brooke, George
 1984 'The Feast of New Wine and the Question of Fasting', *ET* 95: 175-76.
 1988a 'The Temple Scroll and the Archaeology of Qumran, 'Ain Feshka and Masada' (11QTemple)', *RQ* 13: 225-37.
 1988b 'The Temple Scroll: A Law unto Itself?', in B. Lindars (ed.), *Law and Religion: Essays on the Place of the Law in Israel and Early Christianity* (Cambridge: James Clarke): 34-43, 164-66.
 1992a 'The Temple Scroll and LXX Exodus 35-40', in Brooke and Lindars 1992: 81-106.
 1992b 'The Textual Tradition of the Temple Scroll and Recently Published Manuscripts of the Pentateuch', in Dimant and Rappaport 1992: 261-82.
Brooke, George (ed.)
 1989 *Temple Scroll Studies: Papers Presented at the International Symposium on the Temple Scroll, Manchester, December, 1987* (Sheffield: JSOT Press).
Brooke, George, and F. García Martínez (eds.)
 1994 *New Qumran Texts and Studies: Proceedings of the First Meeting of the International Organization for Qumran Studies Paris 1992* (Leiden: E.J. Brill).
Brooke, George, and B. Lindars (eds.)
 1992 *Septuagint, Scrolls and Cognate Writings: Papers Presented to the International Symposium on the Septuagint and its Relations to the Dead Sea Scrolls and Other Writings* (Atlanta, GA: Scholars Press).
Broshi, Magen
 1992a *The Damascus Document Reconsidered* (Jerusalem: Israel Exploration Society).
 1992b 'The Gigantic Dimensions of the Visionary Temple in the Temple Scroll', in Shanks 1992: 113-15.
 1995 'Visionary Architecture and Town Planning in the Dead Sea Scrolls', in Dimant and Schiffman 1995: 9-22.
Burgmann, Hans
 1989 '11QT: The Sadducean Torah', in Brooke 1989: 257-63.
Callaway, Philip
 1985–87 'Source Criticism of the Temple Scroll: The Purity Laws', *RQ* 12: 213-22.

1988 'The Temple Scroll and the Canonization of Jewish Law (11QTemple)', *RQ* 13: 239-50.
1989 'Extending Divine Revelation: Micro-Compositional Strategies in the Temple Scroll', in Brooke 1989: 149-62.

Charles, R.H.
1972 *The Book of Jubilees or the Little Genesis* (Jerusalem: Makor Press).

Charlesworth, James H.
1985 'The Date of Jubilees and of the Temple Scroll', in Kent Harold Richards (ed.), *SBL Seminar Papers*, 24 (Chico, CA: Scholars Press): 192-204.

Chyutin, Michael
1994 'The New Jerusalem: Ideal City', *DSD* 1: 71-97.
1997 *The New Jerusalem Scroll from Qumran: A Comprehensive Reconstruction* (JSPSup, 25; Sheffield: Sheffield Academic Press).

Collins, John J.
1999 'Apocalypticism and Literary Genre in the Dead Sea Scrolls', in Flint and VanderKam 1999: 403-30.

Crawford, Sidnie White (see also Sidnie A. White)
1994 'Three Fragments from Qumran Cave 4 and their Relationship to the "Temple Scroll"', *JQR* 85: 259-73.
1999 'The "Rewritten Bible" at Qumran: A Look at Three Texts', *Eretz Israel* 26: 1-8.

Davies, Philip R.
1989 'The Temple Scroll and the Damascus Document' in Brooke 1989: 201-10.

Delcor, Mathias
1978 *Qumrân: Sa piété, sa théologie et son milieu* (Paris-Gembloux-Leuven: Duculot).
1981 'Le statut du roi d'après le Rouleau de Temple', *Henoch* 3: 47-68.
1989 'Is the Temple Scroll a Source of the Herodian Temple?', in Brooke 1989: 67-89.
1991 'La fête des huttes dans le Rouleau du Temple et dans le livre des Jubilés', *RQ* 15: 181-98.

Dimant, Devorah, and L. Schiffman (eds.)
1995 *Time to Prepare the Way in the Wilderness: Papers on the Qumran Scrolls* (Leiden: E.J. Brill).

Dimant, Devorah, and U. Rappaport (ed.)
1992 *The Dead Sea Scrolls: Forty Years of Research* (Leiden: E.J. Brill).

Duhaime, Jean
1995 'War Scroll' in J.H. Charlesworth (ed.), *The Dead Sea Scrolls: Hebrew, Aramaic and Greek Texts with English Translations*. II. *Damascus Document, War Scroll, and Related Documents* (Tübingen: J.C.B. Mohr): 80-141.

Eisenman, Robert, and Michael Wise
1992 *The Dead Sea Scrolls Uncovered* (Harmondsworth: Penguin Books).

Fabry, Heinz-Josef
1997 'Der Begriff "Tora" in der Tempelrolle', *RQ* 18: 63-77.

Fishbane, Michael
1985 *Biblical Interpretation in Ancient Israel* (Oxford: Oxford University Press).
1986 'Inner Biblical Exegesis: Types and Strategies of Interpretation in Ancient Israel', in G. Hartman and S. Budick (eds.), *Midrash and Literature* (New Haven, CT: Yale University Press): 19-40.

Fitzmyer, Joseph A., S. J.
1990 *The Dead Sea Scrolls: Major Publications and Tools for Study* (SBL Resources for Biblical Study, 20; rev. edn; Atlanta, GA: Scholars Press).

Fitzmyer, Joseph, and Daniel Harrington (eds.)
    1978   *A Manual of Palestinian Aramaic Texts (Second Century BC–Second Century AD)* (Rome: Biblical Institute Press).
Flint, Peter, and J. VanderKam (eds.)
    1998, 1999   *The Dead Sea Scrolls after Fifty Years: A Comprehensive Assessment* (2 vols.; Leiden: E.J. Brill).
García Martínez, Florentino
    1986   'El rollo del Templo (11QTemple): Bibliografia sistemática', *RQ* 12: 425-40.
    1992a   '11QTemple^b: A Preliminary Publication', in Trebolle Barrera and Vegas Montaner 1992: 363-90.
    1992b   'The Last Surviving Columns of 11QNJ', in F. García Martínez *et al.* (eds.), *The Scriptures and the Scrolls: Studies in Honour of A.S. van der Woude on the Occasion of his 65th Birthday* (VTSup, 49; Leiden: E.J. Brill): 178-92.
    1992c   'The "New Jerusalem" and the Future Temple of the Manuscripts from Qumran', in *idem, Qumran and Apocalyptic: Studies on the Aramaic Texts from Qumran* (Leiden: E.J. Brill): 180-213.
    1992d   *Textos de Qumrán* (Madrid: Editorial Trotta).
    1992e   'Texts from Cave 11', in Dimant and Rappaport 1992: 18-26.
    1994   *The Dead Sea Scrolls Translated: The Qumran Texts in English* (trans. W. Watson; Leiden: E.J. Brill).
    1996   'A Classified Bibliography', in Qimron 1996: 93-122.
    1998   'More Fragments of 11QNJ', in D. Parry and E. Ulrich (eds.), *The Provo International Conference on the Dead Sea Scrolls: New Texts, Reformulated Issues, and Technological Innovations* (Leiden: E.J. Brill): 186-98.
    1999   'The Temple Scroll and the New Jerusalem', in Flint and VanderKam 1999: 431-60.
García Martínez, Florentino, and D.W. Parry
    1996   *Bibliography of the Finds in the Desert of Judah 1970–1995* (STDJ, 19; Leiden: E.J. Brill).
García Martínez, Florentino, and E.J.C. Tigchelaar
    1997, 1998   *The Dead Sea Scrolls Study Edition* (2 vols.; Leiden: E.J. Brill).
García Martínez, F., E.J.C. Tigchelaar and A.S. van der Woude (eds.)
    1998   *Qumran Cave 11, II: 11Q2-18, 11Q20-31* (DJD, 23; Oxford: Clarendon Press).
Ginzberg, Louis
    1976   *An Unknown Jewish Sect* (New York: Ktav).
Glessmer, Uwe
    1999   'Calendars in the Qumran Scrolls', in Flint and VanderKam 1999: 213-78.
Grabbe, Lester
    1997   '4QMMT and Second Temple Jewish Society', in Bernstein, García Martínez and Kampen 1997: 89-108.
Greenfield, Jonas
    1969   'The Small Caves of Qumran', *JAOS* 89: 132-35.
Hempel, Charlotte
    1998   *The Laws of the Damascus Document: Sources, Traditions and Redaction* (Leiden: E.J. Brill).
    2000   *The Damascus Texts* (Sheffield: Sheffield Academic Press).
Hengel, Martin, James H. Charlesworth and Doron Mendels
    1986   'The Polemical Character of "On Kingship" in the Temple Scroll: An Attempt at Dating 11QTemple', *JJS* 37: 28-38.

Himmelfarb, Martha
    1999   'Sexual Relations and Purity in the Temple Scroll and the Book of Jubilees', *DSD* 6: 11-36.
Japhet, Sara
    1993   'The Prohibition of the Habitation of Women: The Temple Scroll's Attitude toward Sexual Impurity and its Biblical Precedents', *JANES* 22: 69-87.
Jongeling, Bernard
    1970   'Publication provisoire d'un fragment provenant de la grotte 11 de Qumrân (11QJérNouv ar)', *JSJ* 1: 58-64.
    1979-81   'A propos de la Colonne XXIII du Rouleau du Temple', *RQ* 10: 593-95.
Kaufman, Stephen
    1982   'The Temple Scroll and Higher Criticism', *HUCA* 53: 29-43.
Lemaire, Andre
    1996   'Nouveaux fragments du Rouleau du Temple de Qumrân', *RQ* 17: 271-74.
Levine, Baruch
    1978   'The Temple Scroll: Aspects of its Historical Provenance and Literary Character', *BASOR* 232: 5-23.
    1990   'A Further Look at the Mo'adim of the Temple Scroll', in Schiffman (ed.) 1990: 53-66.
Licht, Jacob
    1979   'An Ideal Town Plan from Qumran: The Description of the New Jerusalem', *IEJ* 29: 45-59.
Magness, Jodi
    1998a   'Qumran Archaeology: Past Perspectives and Future Prospects', in Flint and VanderKam 1998: 47-78.
    1998b   'Two Notes on the Archaeology of Qumran', *BASOR* 312: 37-44.
Maier, Johann
    1978   *Die Tempelrolle vom Toten Meer: Übersetzt und erläutert* (Munich: Reinhardt).
    1985   *The Temple Scroll: An Introduction, Translation and Commentary* (trans. R. White; Sheffield: JSOT Press).
    1989   'The Architectural History of the Temple in Jerusalem in the Light of the Temple Scroll', in Brooke 1989: 23-62.
Mendels, Doron
    1979   ' "On Kingship" in the Temple Scroll and the Ideological Vorlage of the Seven Banquets in the "Letter of Aristeas to Philocrates" ', *Aegyptus* 59: 127-36.
Milgrom, Jacob
    1978a   ' "Sabbath" and "Temple City" in the Temple Scroll', *BASOR* 232: 25-27.
    1978b   'Studies in the Temple Scroll', *JBL* 97: 501-23.
    1978c   'The Temple Scroll', *BA* 41: 105-20.
    1983   'The Shoulder for the Levites' in Yadin 1983: 169-76.
    1984   'New Temple Festivals in the Temple Scroll', in T. Madsen (ed.), *The Temple in Antiquity: Ancient Records and Modern Perspectives* (Provo, UT: Brigham Young University Press): 125-33.
    1989   'The Qumran Cult: Its Exegetical Principles', in Brooke 1989: 165-80.
    1991   'Deviations from Scripture in the Purity Laws of the Temple Scroll', in S. Talmon (ed.), *Jewish Civilization in the Hellenistic-Roman Period* (Sheffield: JSOT Press): 159-67.
    1992   'First Day Ablutions in Qumran', in Trebolle Barrera and Vegas Montaner 1992: 561-70.
    1993–94   'Qumran's Biblical Hermeneutics: The Case of the Wood Offering', *RQ* 16: 449-56.

1993a	'The Concept of Impurity in Jubilees and the Temple Scroll', *RQ* 16: 277-84.
1993b	'On the Purification Offering in the Temple Scroll', *RQ* 16: 99-101.
1994	'The City of the Temple', *JQR* 83: 125-28.

Milik, Jozef T.
1955a	'1QJubilees^a' and 1QJubilees^b', in Barthélemy and Milik 1955: 82-84, pl. xvi.
1955b	'Description de la Jérusalem Nouvelle (?)', in Barthélemy and Milik 1955: 134-35, pl. xxxi.
1962a	'Description de la Jérusalem Nouvelle', in Baillet, Milik and de Vaux 1962: 184-92, pls. xl-xli.
1962b	'Document de Damas', in Baillet, Milik and de Vaux 1962: 181, pl. xxxviii.

Milik, Jozef T., and M. Black
1976	*The Book of Enoch: Aramaic Fragments of Qumran Cave 4* (Oxford: Clarendon Press).

Mink, Hans Aage
1982–84	'Die Kol. III der Tempelrolle. Versuch einer Rekonstruktion', *RQ* 11: 163-81.
1987	'The Use of Scripture in the Temple Scroll and the Status of the Scroll as Law', *Scandinavian Journal of the Old Testament* 20-50.

Murphy-O'Connor, Jerome
1992	'Teacher of Righteousness', in D.N. Freedman (ed.), *The Anchor Bible Dictionary* (6 vols.; New York: Doubleday): VI, 340-41.

Neusner, J., E. Frerich, and N. Sarna (eds.)
1989	*From Ancient Israel to Modern Judaism: Intellect in Quest of Understanding. Essays in Honor of Marvin Fox* (4 vols.; Atlanta, GA: Scholars Press).

Ploeg, J.P.M. van der
1978	'Une halakha inédite de Qumrân', in Delcor 1978: 107-13.
1985	'Les manuscrits de la Grotte XI de Qumrân', *RQ* 12: 9.

Puech, Emile
1995	'A propos de la Jérusalem Nouvelle d'après les manuscrits de la mer Morte', *Semitica* 43-44: 87-102.
1997	'Fragments du plus ancien exemplaire du Rouleau du Temple (4Q524)', in Bernstein, García Martínez and Kampen 1997: 19-64.
1998	'4QRouleau du Temple', in *idem*, *Qumrân Grotte 4, XVIII: Textes hébreux (4Q521-4Q528, 4Q576-4Q579)* (DJD, 25; Oxford: Clarendon Press): 85-114, pls. vii-viii.

Qimron, Elisha
1978a	'New Readings in the Temple Scroll', *IEJ* 28: 161-72.
1978b	'The Text of the Temple Scroll', *Leshonenu* 42: 136-45 (Hebrew).
1981–82	'Three Notes on the Text of the Temple Scroll', *Tarbiz* 51: 135-37 (Hebrew).
1983	'Textual Notes on the Temple Scroll', *Tarbiz* 53: 139-41 (Hebrew).
1987	'Further New Readings in the Temple Scroll', *IEJ* 37: 31-35.
1988	'Column 14 of the Temple Scroll', *IEJ* 38: 44-46.
1996	*The Temple Scroll: A Critical Edition with Extensive Reconstructions* (Beer Sheva: Ben-Gurion University of the Negev Press; Jerusalem: Israel Exploration Society).

Qimron, Elisha, and J. Strugnell
1994	*Miqṣat Ma'aśē ha-Torah: Qumran Cave 4, V* (DJD, 10; Oxford: Clarendon Press).

Rokeah, David
 1983 'The Temple Scroll, Philo, Josephus and the Talmud', *JTS* 34: 515-26.

Schechter, Solomon
 1910 *Documents of Jewish Sectaries*. I. *Fragments of a Zadokite Work* (Cambridge: Cambridge University Press).

Schiffman, Lawrence H.
- 1980   'The Temple Scroll in Literary and Philological Perspective', in W. Green (ed.), *Approaches to Ancient Judaism* (5 vols.; Chico, CA: Scholars Press): II, 143-58.
- 1985   'The Sacrificial System of the Temple Scroll and the Book of Jubilees', *SBL Seminar Papers*, 24 (Chico, CA: Scholars Press): 217-233.
- 1986   'Exclusion from the Sanctuary and the City of the Sanctuary in the Temple Scroll', in R. Ahroni (ed.), *Biblical and Other Studies in Memory of Shelomo D. Goitein* (Columbus, OH: Ohio State University Press): 301-20.
- 1987   The King, his Guard and the Royal Council in the Temple Scroll', *PAAJR* 54: 237-59.
- 1988   'The Laws of War in the Temple Scroll', *RQ* 13: 299-311.
- 1989a   'Architecture and Law: The Temple and its Courtyards in the Temple Scroll', in J. Neusner, E. Frerichs, N. Sarna (eds.), *From Ancient Israel to Modern Judaism: Intellect in Quest of Understanding. Essays in Honor of Marvin Fox*, II (Atlanta, GA: Scholars Press): 267-84.
- 1989b   'The Law of the Temple Scroll and its Provenance', *FO* 25: 85-98.
- 1989c   'Shelamim Sacrifices in the Temple Scroll', *Eretz Israel* 10: 176-83.
- 1989d   'The Temple Scroll and the Systems of Jewish Law of the Second Temple Period', in Brooke 1989: 239-55.
- 1989–90   'Miqsat Ma'aseh ha-Torah and the Temple Scroll', *RQ* 14: 435-57.
- 1990a   'The Impurity of the Dead in the Temple Scroll', in Schiffman (ed.) 1990: 135-57.
- 1990b   'The New Halakhic Letter (4QMMT) and the Origins of the Dead Sea Sect', *BA* 53: 64-73.
- 1990c   'The Prohibition of the Skins of Animals in the Temple Scroll and Miqsat Ma'ase Ha-torah', *WCJS* 10: 191-98.
- 1991–92a   'The Deuteronomic Paraphrase of the Temple Scroll', *RQ* 15: 543-67.
- 1991–92b   'The Law of Vows and Oaths (Num. 30, 3-16) in the Zadokite Fragments and the Temple Scroll', *RQ* 15: 199-214.
- 1992a   'The Furnishings of the Temple According to the Temple Scroll', in Trebolle Barrera and Vegas Montaner 1992: 621-34.
- 1992b   'Laws Pertaining to Women in the Temple Scroll', in Dimant and Rappaport 1992: 210-28.
- 1992c   'The Septuagint and the Temple Scroll: Shared "Halakhic" Variants', in Brooke and Lindars 1992: 277-97.
- 1993a   'The New Halakhic Letter (4QMMT) and the Origin of the Dead Sea Sect', in Z. Kapera (ed.), *Mogilany 1989: Papers on the Dead Sea Scrolls Offered in Memory of Jean Carmignac: Part 1, General Research on the Dead Sea Scrolls, Qumran and the New Testament: The Present State of Qumranology* (Cracow: Enigma): 59-70.
- 1993b   'Sacred Space: The Land of Israel in the Temple Scroll', in A. Biran and J. Aviram (eds.), *Biblical Archaeology Today, Proceedings of the Second International Congress on Biblical Archaeology 1990* (Jerusalem: Israel Exploration Society): 398-410.
- 1994a   'The Millû'îm Ceremony in the Temple Scroll', in Brooke and García Martínez 1994: 255-73.

1994b	'Pharisaic and Sadducean Halakhah in Light of the Dead Sea Scrolls: The Case of Tevul Yom', *DSD* 1: 285-99.
1994c	*Reclaiming the Dead Sea Scrolls: The History of Judaism, the Background of Christianity, the Lost Library of Qumran* (Philadelphia: The Jewish Publication Society).
1994d	'The Temple Scroll and the Nature of its Law: The Status of the Question', in Ulrich and VanderKam 1994: 37-55.
1994e	'The Theology of the Temple Scroll', *JQR* 85: 109-23.
1995a	'"ôlâ and ḥaṭṭa't in the Temple Scroll', in D. Wright (ed.), *Pomegranates and Golden Bells: Studies in Biblical, Jewish and Near Eastern Ritual, Law, and Literature in Honor of Jacob Milgrom* (Winona Lake, IN: Eisenbrauns): 39-48.
1995b	'Sacral and Non-Sacral Slaughter According to the Temple Scroll', in Dimant and Schiffman 1995: 69-84.
1996	'The Construction of the Temple According to the Temple Scroll', *RQ* 17: 555-71.
1999	'The House of the Laver in the Temple Scroll', *Eretz Israel* 26: 169-75.

Schiffman, Lawrence H. (ed.)
1990	*Archaeology and History in the Dead Sea Scrolls: The New York University Conference in Memory of Yigael Yadin* (Sheffield: JSOT Press).

Schuller, Eileen
1994	'Women in the Dead Sea Scrolls', in M. Wise (ed.), *Methods of Investigation of the Dead Sea Scrolls and the Khirbet Qumran Site: Present Realities and Future Prospects* (New York: Academy of Sciences): 115-31.

Shanks, Hershel
1992	*Understanding the Dead Sea Scrolls* (New York: Random House).

Shemesh, Aharon
1999	' "Three-Days' Journey from the Temple": The Use of this Expression in the Temple Scroll', *DSD* 6: 126-38.

Starcky, Jean
1977	'Jérusalem et les manuscrits de la mer Morte', *Le monde de la Bible* 1: 38-40.

Stegemann, Hartmut
1988	'The Origins of the Temple Scroll', *VT* 40: 235-56.
1989	'The Literary Composition of the Temple Scroll and its Status at Qumran', in Brooke 1989: 123-48.
1992a	'Is the Temple Scroll a Sixth Book of the Torah—Lost for 2500 Years?', in Shanks 1992: 126-36.
1992b	'The Institutions of Israel in the Temple Scroll', in Dimant and Rappaport 1992: 156-85.

Sukenik, Eleazar
1955	*The Dead Sea Scrolls of the Hebrew University* (Jerusalem: Magnes Press/ Hebrew University).

Swanson, Dwight
1992	'The Use of the Chronicles in 11QT: Aspects of a Relationship', in Dimant and Rappaport 1992: 290-98.
1994	' "A Covenant Just Like Jacob's": The Covenant of 11QT 29 and Jeremiah's New Covenant', in Brooke and García Martínez 1994: 273-86.
1995	*The Temple Scroll and the Bible: The Methodology of 11QT* (Leiden: E.J. Brill).

Talmon, Shemaryahu
1990	'The Calendar of the Covenanters of the Judean Desert', in *idem, The World of Qumran from Within: Collected Studies* (Leiden: E.J. Brill): 147-85.

Thiering, Barbara
 1989 'The Date of the Composition of the Temple Scroll', in Brooke 1989: 99-120.

Trebolle Barrera, Julio, and L. Vegas Montaner (eds.)
 1992 *The Madrid Qumran Congress: Proceedings of the International Congress on the Dead Sea Scrolls, Madrid 18–21 March 1991* (2 vols.; Leiden: E.J. Brill).

Tov, Emanuel
 1982 'The Temple Scroll and Old Testament Textual Criticism', *Eretz Israel* 16: 100-111 (Hebrew).
 1991 'Deut. 12 and 11QTemple LII–LIII: A Contrastive Analysis', *RQ* 15: 169-73.
 1993 *The Dead Sea Scrolls on Microfiche: A Comprehensive Facsimile Edition of the Texts from the Judean Desert* (Leiden: E.J. Brill).

Tov, Emanuel, and S.A. White
 1994 '4QReworked Pentateuch^c', in Attridge, Elgvin *et al.* 1994: 255-318, pls. xxii-xxxii.

Ulrich, Eugene, and J. VanderKam (eds.)
 1994 *The Community of the Renewed Covenant: The Notre Dame Symposium on the Dead Sea Scrolls* (Notre Dame: University of Notre Dame Press).

VanderKam, James C.
 1989 'The Temple Scroll and the Book of Jubilees', in Brooke 1989: 211-36.
 1994 'The Theology of the Temple Scroll: A Response to Lawrence H. Schiffman', *JQR* 85: 129-35.

VanderKam, James C., and J.T. Milik
 1994 'Jubilees', in Attridge, Elgvin *et al.* 1994: 1-186, pls. i-xii.

Vaux, Roland de
 1973 *Archaeology and the Dead Sea Scrolls* (London: Oxford University Press).

Vermes, Geza
 1989 'Bible Interpretation at Qumran', *Eretz Israel* 10: 184-91.
 1997 *The Complete Dead Sea Scrolls in English* (New York: Penguin Books, 4th edn).

Wacholder, Ben Zion
 1983 *The Dawn of Qumran: The Sectarian Torah and the Teacher of Righteousness* (Cincinnati, OH: Hebrew Union College Press).
 1985 'The Relationship between 11QTorah (The Temple Scroll) and the Book of Jubilees: One Single or Two Independent Compositions', in Kent Harold Richards (ed.), *Society of Biblical Literature Seminar Papers*, XX (Chico, CA: Scholars Press): 205-16.
 1991 'The Fragmentary Remains of 11QTorah (Temple Scroll), 11QTorah^b and 11QTorah^c plus 4QparaTorah Integrated with 11QTorah', *HUCA* 62: 1-116.

Weinfeld, Moshe
 1980 'The Royal Guard According to the Temple Scroll', *RB* 87: 394-96.
 1991–92 'God versus Moses in the Temple Scroll—"I do not speak on my own but on God's authority" (Sifre Deut. sec. 5; John 12, 48f)', *RQ* 15: 175-80.

White, Sidnie A. (see also Sidnie White Crawford)
 1994 '4QTemple?', in Attridge, Elgvin *et al.* 1994: 319-334, pls. xxxiii-xxxiv.

Wilson, Andrew, and Lawrence Wills
 1982 'Literary Sources of the Temple Scroll', *HTR* 75: 275-88.

Wintermute, O.S.
 1985 'Jubilees (Second Century BC): A New Translation and Introduction', in J.H. Charlesworth (ed.), *The Old Testament Pseudepigrapha*. II. *Expansions of*

the 'Old Testament' and Legends, Wisdom and Philosophical Literature, Prayers, Psalms and Odes, Fragments of Lost Judeo-Hellenistic Works (Garden City, NY: Doubleday): 35-142.

Wise, Michael
1988   'A New Manuscript Join in the "Festival of Wood Offering" (Temple Scroll XXIII)', *JNES* 47: 113-21.
1989   'The Covenant of the Temple Scroll XXIX, 3-10', *RQ* 14: 49-60.
1990a   *A Critical Study of the Temple Scroll from Qumran Cave 11* (SAOC, 49; Chicago, IL: University of Chicago Press).
1990b   'The Eschatological Vision of the Temple Scroll', *JNES* 49: 155-72.
1993   'Literary Criticism of the Temple Scroll (11QTemple)', *QC* 3: 101-37.

Wise, Michael, M. Abegg and E. Cook (eds.)
1996   *The Dead Sea Scrolls: A New Translation* (New York: HarperCollins).

Woude, A.S. van der
1988   'Ein bisher unveröffentlichtes Fragment der Tempelrolle', *RQ* 13: 89-92.

Yadin, Yigael
1967a   'Un nouveau manuscrit de la mer Morte: "Le Rouleau du Temple"', *CRAIBL*: 607-19.
1967b   'The Temple Scroll', *Nouvelles Chrétiennes d'Israël* 18: 41-8.
1967c   'The Temple Scroll', *BA* 30: 135-39.
1968   'The Temple Scroll', in J. Aviram (ed.), *Jerusalem through the Ages* (Jerusalem: Israel Exploration Society): 72-82.
1969   'De Tempelrol', *Spiegel historiae* 4: 203-10.
1971   'The Temple Scroll', in D.N. Freedman and J.C. Greenfield (eds.), *New Directions in Biblical Archaeology* (Garden City, NY: Doubleday): 156-66.
1977   *Megillat ham-Miqdāš (The Temple Scroll)* (3 vols.; Jerusalem: Israel Exploration Society) (Hebrew).
1978   'Le Rouleau du Temple', in Delcor 1978: 115-19.
1982   'Is the Temple Scroll a Sectarian Document?' in G. Tucker and D. Knight (eds.), *Humanizing America's Iconic Book: Society of Biblical Literature Centennial Addresses 1980* (Chico, CA: Scholars Press): 153-69.
1983   *The Temple Scroll* (3 vols. and supplement; rev. edn; Jerusalem: Israel Exploration Society).
1985   *The Temple Scroll: The Hidden Law of the Dead Sea Sect* (New York: Random House).

INDEXES

INDEX OF REFERENCES

BIBLE

Genesis		15.19-30	44	19.12	44
1–Exod. 15	77	16.2-34	55	19.16	45
24.37-38	59	17.13	20	20.14-21	73
		18.12-14	61, 62, 81	22.1-3	73
Exodus		18.16	61	28–29	50
12.1-13	51	18.18	60	28.3-8	50
19.10-15	46	20.17	61	28.9-10	50
20	27	20.21	61	28.11-15	50
25–30	34	21.14	59	28.26-31	51
25–27	35	22.28	80	29.1-6	50, 55
25	33	23	50	29.7-11	55
25.1-9	33	23.5	51	29.13–30.1	55
25.9	33	23.6-8	51	31.27-30	21
25.10-22	35	23.10-14	51	36.6-8	59
26.31-33	35	23.15-21	51		
29	50	23.15-17	52	*Deuteronomy*	
29.38-42	50	23.15-16	52	5	27
30.14	51	23.23-25	55	7	57
32.1-20	18	23.24–24.2	55	7.3-7	59
34	18, 19, 57	23.26-32	55	7.13	53
34.1-2	18	23.33-36	55	11.14	53
34.16	59	24.5-9	72	12–26	57
36–38	35	27.30	56	12.17	53
40.2	50			12.22-24	20
		Numbers		13.18-19	18
Leviticus		1.2-3	51	14.18	59
8	50	3–4	33	14.22-26	53
8.26-29	51	3.14-39	38	14.23	53
11.24-25	44	5.2-3	47	16.5-7	51
11.29-38	79	5.2	47	17.14-20	58
12.2-8	44	9.2-5	51	17.16	58
12.2-5	47	15.1-13	50	17.17	58
14.8-9	44	18.12	53	18.4	53
15.5-11	44	18.21-24	56	19.17	56
15.16-18	46	19.9	79	21.22-23	60
15.19-31	47	19.10-15	44	21.23	14

Index of References

22.11	14	*2 Chronicles*		*Hosea*	
23.1	61	3–4	34	2.10	53
23.3-6	73	8.11	46	2.24	53
23.10-12	46	30.13	51		
24.1-4	60	31.5	53	*Revelation*	
25.5-9	14	35.1	51	21.9-27	74
27.22	61				
28.51	53	*Ezra*		Pseudepigrapha	
		9–10	59	*1 En.*	
1 Samuel				72–82	83
10.25	59	*Nehemiah*			
21.4-6	46	8.16	55	*4 Ezra*	
30.24-25	21	10.34	54	10.25-28	74
		13.23-29	59		
1 Kings				*Jub.*	
6	34	*Esther*		1.27-28	77
6.19-28	35	7.9-10	61	6.21	78
6.20	35			7.2-3	78
7.30-33	15	*Song of Songs*		21.13-14	78
		3.8	59	27.19	78
2 Kings				29.1	78
18.32	53	*Ezekiel*		29.10-20	78
23.21-23	51	1.15-21	15	29.19	50
25.1-17	73	40–48	34	31–32	57
		43–44	56	31.15	78
1 Chronicles		45.3-4	49	32.3-9	78
4.7-8	36			32.10-15	78
24.7-18	72	*Daniel*		45.15	78
28.9-19	33	11.30	73	49	51
28.19	33				

QUMRAN

1QM		5–8	68	5.i	15
1.1-7	73	7	71	5.ii	15
2.1-6	74				
2.1-3	83	*4Q174*		*4Q524*	
2.1-2	72	1-3.1.2	74	1	14, 34
7.3	83			2	14
7.6-7	83	*4Q365a*		3	14
7.7	42	1	15	4	14
14.2-3	44	2	15, 34	5	14
		2.i	15	6–13	14
2Q24		2.ii	15, 39	14	14
1	68, 69, 71	3–5	15	14.5	14
3	71	3	15, 34	15–22	14, 61
4	68, 69, 71	4	15, 34	23	14
4.9-16	72	5	34		

4Q554		**4QRP^c**		3.4	35
1	68, 69	23	54, 83	3.9	35
1.1–2.7-11	70	23.9-11	55	3.14-17	13
1.1–2.11-22	70	23.9	55	4.9-10	36
1.2.12	70			4.13	35
1.2.15-22	71	**5Q15**		6	12
1.2.15	70	1	68, 69	7.10-12	35
1.2.18	71	1.1-2	71	7.13	35
1.3	71	1.1.3-4	71	8.5-14	35
1.3.20-22	82	1.2-7	71	9.1-14	36
2	68	1.2.11	71	12	38
2.1	68	2.2-5	82	12.8–13.7	50
2.2	68			13–29	14, 29
2.3	68, 73, 74	**11Q18**		13.8–30.2	23
2.3.15-22	73	6	71, 82	13.8	50
		8	71	13.9–30.2	22, 49
4Q554a		9.1	71	13.10-16	50
8	71	10.1	71	13.17–14.2	50
		11	71	14–66	12
4QDa		12.1	72	14.2-8	50
6.4	81	12.18	72	14.9–15.2	50
12	81	13	71	14.9	78
		14	72	15.03–16.04	13
4QDe		15	72	15.3-10	50
2.2-15	81	15.4	72	16	38
2.2.6-8	81	16.2	72	16.1-3	13
2.2.13	81	19	72, 73	16.8-11	13
2.2.15	81	20.1-7	72	17.6-16	51
2.2.19	81	22	71	17.6-9	78
4	81	27	72	17.13	13
		30	82	18.1-10	51
4QMMT A		31.2	71	18.4-7	13
20	53	31.33	71	18.10–19.9	51
				18.10-13	52
4QMMT B		**11Q19**		19.2-9	13
9–13	79	1–5	12	19.9	78
13–17	79	2–34	14	19.11–21.10	51
18–20	80	2–13	12	19.11-13	52
36–38	80, 81	2	18, 23, 29,	19.12–20.10	13
49–54	80		57	19.13-16	13
62–64	80, 81	2.1–13.8	22, 34	20	68
64–72	79	2.1–15	23, 57	20.11-13	79
72–74	80	3–13	35	21.01–22.5	13
		3–12	29	21.02-05	56
4QNJara		3	38	21.12–23.2	51
1.1-2	40	3.1–13.8	23, 34	21.12-14	52
		3.2	35	22	56, 82

Index of References

22.05-5	13	40.14–41.11	39	50.02-11	13
22.6–23.01	13	41	15	50.4-6	80
22.8-11	56	41.17–42.9	40	50.4	46
22.12	56	42.10-17	40, 55	50.10-16	44
23–25.2	78	42.10	40	50.15–51.1	13
23–24	56, 83	43.4-17	53	50.16	46
23	38	43.4-10	78	50.17-21	14
23.1–25.1	54	43.4-6	20	51	57
24–29	13	44	56	51.2-5	79
25.2-10	55	44.1–45.7a	23	51.3	46
25.10-27	55	44.5	18	51.5-17	13
27	55	45–47	29, 42	51.5b-10	42
27.10–29.1	55	45	42	51.6-7	18
29.2–30.2	23	45.1-4	13	51.10	42
29.2-10	56	45.03-04	13	51.11–56.21	22, 57
29.9-10	74	45.7-8	45	51.11–56.11	29
29.10	50	45.9–46.16	13	51.11-66	57
30–44	29	45.9-10	79	51.11-18	23, 57
30–31	82	45.9	46	52.1-12	23, 57
30	36	45.10	46	52.5-7	80, 81
30.3–47.18	22, 34	45.11-12	45, 48, 81	52.10-12	20
30.3–31.9a	23	45.12-13	80	52.13-16	49
30.5	35	45.17	47	52.18	70
31.10–34.12a	23	46	48	53.1–56.21	23, 57
31.11-13	13	46.1-11a	23	54.4-5	60
32.10-15	13	46.1-4	40	54.5	14
32.12-15	36	46.9-11	41	54.19–55.6	13
34	36	46.13–47.2	23	55.11-14	17
34.15–35.9a	23	46.13	83	55.11-13	14
35	14, 24, 82	46.16–47.3	13	55.11	17
35.7	14, 34	47–51	43	55.12	17
35.10–39.5a	23	47	43	55.13	17
35.10-13	37	47.3-6	49	55.14	17
36–48	14	47.7-18	80	56.1–59.21	57
36	82	47.14-15	49	56.12–59	29
37.9–38.01	13	48–51	24	56.12-21	58
38	15	48.1–51.10	22, 29, 42	56.21	59
38.15	38	48.1-10a	23, 57	57–59	22, 57, 58
39–41	70	48.11-14	45, 49	57	59
39–40	56	48.16	44	57.1–59.21	23
39.6	83	48.18	44	57.1-5	59
39.7-9	45	49–51	44	57.5-11	59
39.8-11	39	49.5-21	47	57.11-15	59
39.11b–40.5	23	49.5	47	57.11-13	83
40	39	49.06-07	14	57.12-15	56
40.5-7	70	49.19-21	79	57.15-19	59, 81
40.7–43.12a	23	49.20	46	57.19-21	59
40.8	39	50–66	24	58.3-21	59

58.10-13	14	*11Q20*		14.26.i	13	
58.11-15	20	1.1	13	14.27	13	
59.2-21	59	1.2	13	14.28	13	
59.9-11	59	3.4	13	14.29	13	
59.17–60.6	14	3.5	13	15.26.ii	13	
60–67	29	3.6	13	16.30	13	
60.1–66.17	22, 57	3.7	13			
60.2-11	23, 57	3.i	13	*11Q21*		
60.2-4	80, 81	3.ii	13	1	13	
60.6-9	56	4.8	13	2	13	
60.6-7	56	4.9	13	3	13	
60.12–63.14a	23, 57	5.10.i	13	3.2	13	
61.8-9	56	5.11	13	3.4	13	
63.10-15	81	6.10.ii	13	3.5	13	
64.1-6a	23, 57	6.12	13			
64.6-13	60	7.13	13	*11Q29*		
64.6-11	14	8.14	13	17.2-4	14	
64.6-9	81	9.15	13			
64.6b-13a	23, 57	9.16	13	*CD*		
64.11b–65.07	14	10.17	13	3.21–4.12	81	
64.13b–66.9b	23, 57	11.18	13	4.20–5.5	81	
65.7	14	11.19	13	4.20-21	60	
66	20, 61	11.20	13	5.7-11	28, 62, 81	
66.8-17	14	12.21.i	13	10.14–11.18	81	
66.10-12a	23, 57	12.22	13	12.1-2	45, 48, 81	
66.11-17	61	12.23	13	13.3-7	81	
66.12-17	60	12.24	13	16.2b-4a	77, 81	
66.15-17	81	13.21.ii	13	19.34-35	28	
66.16-17	27	13.25	13	20.13-15	28	
67	14					

OTHER ANCIENT REFERENCES

Mishnah		3.5	37	Josephus	
Ḥul.		4.6	40	*Ant.*	
4.3	45			13.373	38
		Yom.			
Ma'as. Š.		5.6	36	*War*	
5.3	80			2.147-49	42
		Zeb.		5.224	40
Men.		5.8	80		
1.3-4	79			Eusebius	
9.6	50	Talmud		*Praep. Evang.*	
		b. Ḥul.		451	40
Mid.		72a	45		
2.1	38				

INDEX OF AUTHORS

Alon, G. 43

Baumgarten, J. 28, 43, 46, 54, 61
Bean, P. 38, 39, 41
Beyer, K. 74
Boccaccini, G. 28
Brooke, G. 26, 78
Broshi, M. 39, 70, 74, 75, 82

Callaway, P. 22-24, 42, 43
Charlesworth, J.H. 24, 37, 77
Chyutin, M. 69-71, 73, 75
Collins, J.J. 74
Crawford, S.W. 40, 83

Davies, P.R. 7

Fishbane, M. 19

García Martínez, F. 12, 13, 26, 27, 68, 69, 71, 72, 74, 75, 82
Ginzberg, L. 48
Glessmer, U. 53, 72, 79
Grabbe, L.L. 80
Greenfield, J. 74

Hempel, C. 60, 80
Hengel, M. 24, 37
Himmelfarb, M. 44

Japhet, S. 44, 46, 47

Levine, B. 24, 48, 53
Licht, J. 70, 74

Magness, J.M 42, 43
Maier, J. 24, 26, 38
Mendels, D. 24, 37

Milgrom, J. 22, 43, 44, 46, 48-50, 52, 56, 69
Milik, J.T. 70
Mink, H.A. 26, 27
Murphy-O'Connor, J. 26

Ploeg, J. van der 69
Puech, E. 14, 15, 24, 26, 34, 61, 68, 70, 75

Qimron, E. 12, 15, 78, 79

Schiffman, L.H. 18, 24, 27-29, 34, 38, 40, 43-46, 48, 50, 55, 57, 59, 79, 80, 83
Stegemann, H. 24, 25, 53, 55, 83
Strugnell, J. 15, 78, 79
Swanson, D. 22, 25, 42, 43, 44, 57

Thiering, B. 83
Tigchelaar, E.J.C. 13, 69, 72
Tov, E. 15, 22, 54, 55

VanderKam, J.C. 25, 29, 78, 82
Vaux, R. de 11, 15, 42
Vermes. G. 18

Wacholder, B.Z. 15, 23, 24, 26-28, 48, 57, 78
White, S.A. 15, 34, 39, 54, 55
Wills, L. 22, 23, 34, 42, 43, 49, 57
Wilson, A. 22, 23, 34, 42, 43, 49, 57
Wise, M. 23, 26, 28, 40, 43, 44, 49, 55, 57-59, 61, 70, 74, 75, 82, 83
Woude, A.S. van der 13, 69, 72

Yadin, Y. 11, 12, 15, 16, 19, 21, 24-28, 33, 35-41, 44-53, 55, 57-61, 83

www.ingramcontent.com/pod-product-compliance
Lightning Source LLC
Chambersburg PA
CBHW061420300426
44114CB00015B/2011